A Parent's Guide to the Common Core

Grade 4

© 2014 Kaplan, Inc.

Published by Kaplan Publishing, a division of Kaplan, Inc.
395 Hudson Street
New York, NY 10014

Printed in the United States of America

10 9 8 7 6 5 4 3 2 1

ISBN-13: 978-1-61865-821-0

Kaplan Publishing books are available at special quantity discounts to use for sales promotions, employee premiums, or educational purposes. For more information or to purchase books, please call the Simon & Schuster special sales department at 866-506-1949.

TABLE OF CONTENTS

V. Mathematics

VI. Post-tests: English Language Arts and Mathematics

INTRODUCTION TO THE COMMON CORE STANDARDS

This book is designed to introduce you and your child to the Common Core Standards, a major development in the way U.S. students are taught the most basic and critical areas of knowledge that they will encounter while in school. The Common Core Standards will be used to create assessments beginning in the 2014-2015 school year.

Where did the Common Core Standards come from?

The Common Core Standards were developed to create more uniform academic standards across the United States. Since each state has traditionally created its own academic standards and assessments, students in one state would often end up studying different things than students in another state. Education professionals from across the nation worked together to select the best and most relevant standards from all the states, and then used these as the basis for new standards that could be used by every state to ensure that all students are fully prepared for the future. The Common Core Standards are, in many cases, more comprehensive and demanding than previous state standards. These new standards are designed to help American students perform favorably against students from other developed nations—an area in which the United States has fallen behind in recent years.

The Common Core Standards were not created by the federal government. Each state may choose whether it wishes to use the Common Core Standards, or stick with its own unique learning standards. However, most states have recognized the importance of consistent and high-level standards for all American students. At printing, forty-five states, along with the District of Columbia and four U.S. territories, have adopted the Common Core Standards.

What are the Common Core Standards?

The Common Core Standards are the standards to which all students will be held. These standards are applicable for grades K-12. The Common Core Standards focus on two areas of learning: English Language Arts and Mathematics. These areas were chosen because they are critical to developing a solid foundation for learning, and encompass other fields such as social studies and science.

Within English Language Arts, the Common Core Standards are divided into several categories: Reading; Writing; Speaking & Listening; and Language. For Grade 4, reading standards are focused on finding main ideas, understanding arguments, and identifying story elements in reading passages. Writing standards focus on developing arguments that are supported with evidence and information. These skills are critical for building a foundation for success, both in school and in later life.

Within Mathematics, the Common Core Standards are also divided into several categories. For Grade 4, these categories are: Operations & Algebraic Thinking; Number & Operations in Base Ten; Number & Operations—Fractions; Measurement & Data; and Geometry. For Grade 4, Operations & Algebraic Thinking focuses mainly on completing multi-step word problems. Number & Operations—Fractions focuses on adding, subtracting, and multiplying fractions. Number & Operations in Base Ten focuses on multi-digit multiplication and division using area models to illustrate these principles. These skills have been identified as critical for success in other areas such as the sciences.

The Common Core Standards do not dictate a teacher's curriculum; they just ensure that all teachers are working toward the same learning standards. Teachers were instrumental in developing the standards, and remain the dominant force in helping your child achieve academic potential. However, as a parent, you now have the opportunity to see the "road map" that your child's teachers will be using to build their courses of study. This allows you to better become an active participant in helping your child achieve these learning goals.

How to use this book

This book is designed to provide you with the tools necessary to help your child succeed. While the Common Core Standards are numerous for each grade level, Kaplan's learning experts have identified the standards that are most critical for success, both in the classroom and on assessment tests. These are known as the "power standards." Each lesson in this book is dedicated to a different power standard. The power standards are also the focus of the tests and quizzes throughout the book.

You should begin by having your child take the Pre-Test for each domain. The Pre-Test is designed to cover the same skills that will likely be tested on state assessments. This will give you an idea of the areas in which your child excels, as well as the areas that may need special attention.

Once you have gauged your child's baseline skills, the lessons offer practical experience with each of the power standards. Each lesson provides information on what the standard means, and offers examples of how the standard might be addressed through classroom teaching and through testing. In addition, each lesson offers an activity that you can engage in with your child to help practice the skills highlighted in the lesson. Once you are confident in your child's abilities with regard to a lesson, you can have your child take the end-of-lesson quiz for that power standard to ensure mastery.

When you have completed all the lessons, have your child complete the Post-Test for each domain. You can compare your child's performance on the Post-Test to the Pre-Test, and see which areas have improved the most. If some areas still need work, re-read the corresponding lesson with your child, and try to pinpoint the specific issue that your child needs additional help mastering. The List of Resources provided with this book includes a number of Web sites, publications, and other types of resources that can help you and your child continue to practice and reinforce the Common Core Standards.

Common Core State Standards Initiative http://www.corestandards.org/.
This Web site offers in-depth information about the Common Core Standards and their history.

National Library of Virtual Manipulatives http://nlvm.usu.edu/en/nav/vlibrary.html.
This National Science Foundation supported project allows students, teachers, and parents to interact with virtual manipulatives that can aid in teaching basic mathematic principles.

Learning Resources Shop: Math Manipulatives http://www.learningresources.com/category/teachers /shop+by+category/manipulatives/math.do.
This educational supplier offers a variety of manipulatives that can be used by you and your child to master basic math concepts.

Math Videos by Math Playground http://www.mathplayground.com/mathvideos.html.
These videos address a wide range of math-related questions, from "How do you add fractions?" to "How do you solve an inequality?"

Inside Mathematics: http://www.insidemathematics.org/.
This invaluable resource, intended primarily for educators, includes tools for teaching math as well as a section addressing the Common Core Standards.

New Common Core Math Problems and Resources https://www.khanacademy.org/commoncore.
Khan Academy, one of the world's premier not-for-profit online classrooms, offers practice problems that are mapped to the specific Common Core Standards and organized by grade level.

Illustrative Mathematics: http://www.illustrativemathematics.org/4.
This site offers examples to illustrate the Common Core Standards for every grade level.

Free Activities and Worksheets from Flashkids http://www.flashkids.com/free-downloads.
These activities and worksheets are broken down by domain and grade level, and can be a fun way to improve skills critical to Common Core.

Parents' Guide to Student Success, 4th Grade: http://pta.org/files/4th%20Grade_B-W.pdf.
This overview from the National Parent-Teacher Association tells you in detail what you should expect from a curriculum aimed at meeting Common Core Standards.

Parent Roadmaps to the Common Core Standards—English Language Arts http://www.cgcs.org /Domain/36.

The Council of the Great City Schools offers parent roadmaps to help you support your child in math and English language arts at each grade level.

Working with the "Shifts" http://www.engageny.org/sites/default/files/resource/attachments/parent _workshop_what_parents_can_do_handout.pdf.
This handout from the New York State Education Department explains in detail how the Common Core Standards have shifted the content and methods used by teachers, and offers suggestions for how you can help your student thrive amid these changes.

Achieve the Core http://www.achievethecore.org/.
This Web site was created by the main creators of the Common Core Standards as a way to provide free teaching materials tailored to help students master the skills needed to meet these standards.

ReadWriteThink Tips & How-To Resources for Parents http://www.readwritethink.org/search/?grade =8-12&resource_type=74.
This site, supported by the International Reading Association and the National Council of Teachers of English, provides tips to help parents nurture their child's interest in reading and the language arts.

PBS Parents: Reading & Language: http://www.pbs.org/parents/education/reading-language/.
This Web site, affiliated with the Public Broadcasting Service (PBS), offers advice for improving your child's literacy and love of reading.

The Children of Odin: The Book of Northern Myths by Padraic Colum.
This collection of Norse myths, available in the public domain, is an excellent text for fourth-grade readers. The fourth-grade ELA standards specifically identify familiarity with characters from mythology as a testable component.

American Library Association Summer Reading List, Grades 3-5 http://www.ala.org/alsc/sites/ala .org.alsc/files/content/SummerReadingList_3-5_BW.pdf.
This list, aimed at keeping kids involved in reading during their summer months, includes titles that are highly recommended by student readers at the same grade level as your child.

ENGLISH LANGUAGE ARTS PRE-TEST

The pre-test is intended as a preliminary assessment of your child's language arts skills. The questions cover reading comprehension, vocabulary, and writing. There are a variety of question types at various levels of cognition. These are typical of the types of questions that your fourth grader might experience in the classroom, as homework, and in assessment situations.

A grid at the end provides the main Common Core standard assessed, as well as a brief explanation of the correct answers. This is intended to provide information about which standards your child might need the most help with. Because of this, you may want to encourage your child to take an educated guess on questions that he or she is unsure of, but to mark these also with a question mark. This will help you identify areas that might need some reinforcement.

The items on the pre-test are **not** designed to replicate standardized tests used to assess a child's reading level or a school's progress in helping the child achieve grade level.

Read the following two paragraphs aloud to your child:

This test includes questions to test reading and writing skills. Please answer as best as possible. The test will not be graded. If you come across a question that you are unsure of, put a question mark next to it and make your best guess.

Some of the questions are based on stories or other reading passages. Read the passage carefully. If you don't know the answer to a question, look back at the passage to see if you can find it.

Directions: For each section, read the passage and then answer the questions that follow.

 ## Oney Judge

Oney Judge was a slave who was owned by President George Washington and his wife Martha. She was born around 1773 at the Washington family's plantation in Virginia, which was known as Mount Vernon. Her mother was a slave, and her father was an indentured servant. Indentured servants were similar to slaves, but they were freed as soon as their financial debts were paid off. As the daughter of a slave, however, Oney was also considered by law to be a slave and became the property of the Washingtons.

When George Washington became president in 1789, he brought several of his slaves to work in the presidential house in New York City, which was considered the nation's capital at that time. The following year, the capital was moved to Philadelphia, so Washington and his slaves moved there. Pennsylvania was less supportive of slavery than Virginia. The state passed laws abolishing future slavery, and also held that if a slave spent more than six months living in Pennsylvania, he or she could establish residency there and be considered free. Washington and other government officials objected to this law, since they were required to live in Philadelphia to perform their duties. To keep his slaves from claiming their freedom, Washington transferred his household slaves in Philadelphia back to Mount Vernon every six months, and brought some of his Mount Vernon slaves to Philadelphia.

In 1796, while she was working at the presidential household, Oney decided to run away. She did not want to be sent back to Virginia. Instead, she headed north to New Hampshire, where other free blacks and opponents of slavery helped to hide her. Washington tried to have Oney brought back by force, but he was told that kidnapping Oney would likely cause a riot among those who supported her fight for freedom. Eventually, Washington gave up on trying to reclaim Oney as a slave. When he died, Washington's will left instructions to free the slaves he owned after his wife's death. Martha freed her husband's slaves within a year of his death. However, Oney was considered the property of Martha Washington, and was never freed. She lived as a fugitive in New Hampshire until she was seventy-five years old and became a famous figure in the movement to end slavery.

Questions

1. Why was Oney considered by law to be a slave?

   _____

   _____

2. Based on its usage in the second paragraph, which of the following is closest in meaning to the word *abolishing*?
   A. *strengthening*   C. *making shiny*
   B. *making legal*   D. *putting an end to*

3. Which of the following is evidence that Pennsylvania was not supportive of slavery?
   A. *The nation's capital was located in Philadelphia.*
   B. *The state allowed slaves to establish residency.*
   C. *The state told Washington to free all slaves.*
   D. *The state was located north of Virginia.*

4. Write a brief summary of this passage.

   _____

   _____

   _____

   _____

5. Based on the passage, which of the following statements is most likely to be true?
   A. *George Washington preferred Philadelphia to Virginia.*
   B. *Mount Vernon was the largest plantation in Virginia in the 1790s.*
   C. *New Hampshire did not support slavery in the 1790s.*
   D. *Indentured servants were more common than slaves in the 1790s.*

6. Based on its usage in the third paragraph, which of the following is closest in meaning to the word *fugitive*?
   A. *slave*　　　　B. *farmer*　　　　C. *friend*　　　　D. *runaway*

7. How did Washington prevent his slaves from establishing residency in Pennsylvania?

   _____

   _____

8. According to the passage, where did Oney Judge live after escaping from the Washingtons?
   A. *New York*　　　　　　　C. *Pennsylvania*
   B. *New Hampshire*　　　　D. *Virginia*

9. According to the passage, why did Washington give up on trying to reclaim Oney Judge?
   A. *He feared it would cause a riot.*
   B. *He decided slavery was wrong.*
   C. *He was too busy serving as president.*
   D. *He could not find her.*

10. In your opinion, is there evidence in the passage that Washington did not fully support slavery?

   _____

   _____

 ## *Call of the Wild* by Jack London (excerpt)

Buck lived at a big house in the sun-kissed Santa Clara Valley. Judge Miller's place, it was called. It stood back from the road, half hidden among the trees, through which glimpses could be caught of the wide cool veranda that ran around its four sides. The house was approached by gravelled driveways which wound about through wide-spreading lawns and under the interlacing boughs of tall poplars. At the rear things were on even a more spacious scale than at the front. There were great stables, where a dozen grooms and boys held forth, rows of vine-clad servants' cottages, an endless and orderly array of outhouses, long grape arbors, green pastures, orchards, and berry patches. Then there was the pumping plant for the artesian well, and the big cement tank where Judge Miller's boys took their morning plunge and kept cool in the hot afternoon.

And over this great demesne Buck ruled. Here he was born, and here he had lived the four years of his life. It was true, there were other dogs. There could not but be other dogs on so vast a place, but they did not count. They came and went, resided in the populous kennels, or lived obscurely in the recesses of the house after the fashion of Toots, the Japanese pug, or Ysabel, the Mexican hairless,—strange creatures that rarely put nose out of doors or set foot to ground. On the other hand, there were the fox terriers, a score of them at least, who yelped fearful promises at Toots and Ysabel looking out of the windows at them and protected by a legion of housemaids armed with brooms and mops.

But Buck was neither house-dog nor kennel-dog. The whole realm was his. He plunged into the swimming tank or went hunting with the Judge's sons; he escorted Mollie and Alice, the Judge's daughters, on long twilight or early morning rambles; on wintry nights he lay at the Judge's feet before the roaring library fire; he carried the Judge's grandsons on his back, or rolled them in the grass, and guarded their footsteps through wild adventures down to the fountain in the stable yard, and even beyond, where the paddocks were, and the berry patches. Among the terriers he stalked imperiously, and Toots and Ysabel he utterly ignored, for he was king,—king over all creeping, crawling, flying things of Judge Miller's place, humans included.

? Questions

11. Based on the details in the passage, which of the following statements about Buck is true?
    A. Buck is Judge Miller's son.
    B. Buck is Judge Miller's dog.
    C. Buck is Judge Miller's horse.
    D. Buck is a farm hand who works for Judge Miller.

12. Based on its usage in the first paragraph, which of the following is closest in meaning to the word *boughs*?
    A. branches   B. bends over   C. weapons   D. calls out

13. According to the passage, how old is Buck?
    A. two years old   C. ten years old
    B. four years old   D. twenty years old

14. Write a brief summary of the passage.

    _____

    _____

    _____

15. According the passage, how does Buck respond to the small house dogs?

    _____

    _____

16. Based on its usage in the second paragraph, which of the following is closest in meaning to the word *demesne*?
    A. section of land   C. type of tree
    B. group of animals   D. fountain

17. According to the passage, what are the names of Judge Miller's daughters?
    A. Toots and Ysabel   C. Clara and Mollie
    B. Mollie and Alice   D. Clara and Alice

18. Which of the following is evidence that Buck is king over all things at Judge Miller's place?
    A. He is much larger and stronger than the house-dogs.
    B. He was born at Judge Miller's place.
    C. He can go anywhere he wants, unlike other animals.
    D. He can hunt better than the fox terriers.

19. Based on its usage in the second paragraph, which of the following is closest in meaning to the word *legion*?
    A. large group   C. hunting weapon
    B. mythical tale   D. hunting dog

20. Use your own words to write a paragraph describing Buck. Use details from the story. Use correct grammar, punctuation, spelling, and capitalization.

    _____

    _____

    _____

    _____

Read the paragraph and decide on the best word to fill each blank.
    (1) People _____ not usually think about where their trash goes when it is picked up. (2) I did not think about it either until I _____ walking to school last Tuesday and I saw the trash guys picking up garbage. (3) I walked up to _____ truck and asked them where they took it all. (4) They said it goes _____ a dump outside of town. (5) But what _____ in the future when the dump is too full?

21. In sentence 1, which word is the best choice to fill the blank?
    A. does   B. do   C. didn't   D. doing

22. In sentence 2, which word is the best choice to fill the blank?
    A. am   B. is   C. were   D. was

23. In sentence 3, which word is the best choice to fill the blank?
    A. their   B. they're   C. there   D. these

24. In sentence 4, which word is the best choice to fill the blank?
    A. at   B. with   C. from   D. to

25. In sentence 5, which word is the best choice to fill the blank?
    A. happen   B. happened   C. happens   D. happening

26. Read this draft of a paragraph. Correct the grammar, punctuation, spelling, and capitalization.

Many think that peopel my age watch too much TV. Though I enjoy many shows myself, I agree that people my age overdoes it sometimes. when you watch a lot of TV, your missing out on importent exercise that will keep you health and fit TV can also hurt your eyes, because they need to look at thing's from a distance sometimes to strengthen the eye muscels. Everyone likes TV, but if we can cut down on the amount of TV we watch, we probably feel better.

_____

_____

_____

_____

_____

_____

_____

 Answer Key

Note: The answers to open-ended, constructed response questions are sample answers. Answers will vary, but look for the main ideas to be included.

Highlight any questions that your child gets wrong. Looking at the wrong answers may help to reveal one or more standards with which your child is struggling. Even if your child has done well on this pretest, reviewing the lessons will help him or her become a better reader and writer.

Passage	Question	Answer	Standard(s)
Oney Judge	1	Even though Oney's father was not a slave, her mother was. That made it so she was considered a slave.	RI.4.1
	2	D	RI.4.4
	3	B	RI.4.8. RI.4.1
	4	Oney Judge was an enslaved person owned by George and Martha Washington. Along with the Washingtons' other slaves, Oney moved with the family to New York City when Washington became president. The U.S. capital then moved to Philadelphia. Pennsylvania had laws that said slaves should be freed after six months of living in the state. But Washington came up with a plan to avoid this, so Oney escaped. She was never caught.	RI.4.2
	5	C	RI.4.1
	6	D	RI.4.4
	7	Washington sent his slaves to Virginia every six months.	RI.4.1

Passage	Question	Answer	Standard(s)
	8	B	RI.4.1
	9	A	RI.4.8, RI.4.1
	10	Yes, there is evidence that Washington did not fully support slavery. He indicated that his slaves were to be freed once he and Martha had died. He would not have done this if he had been totally in support of slavery.	RI.4.8, W.4.1
Call of the Wild	11	B	RL.4.1
	12	A	RL.4.4
	13	B	RL.4.1
	14	Buck is a dog who lives on the large estate of Judge Miller. Buck is considered the top dog, above the dogs who live indoors or live in the kennels. Even the people of the house view him that way.	RL.4.2
	15	Buck ignores the small house dogs Toots and Ysabel. He doesn't think much of them.	RL.4.3
	16	A	RL.4.4
	17	B	RL.4.1
	18	C	RL.4.3
	19	A	RL.4.4
	20	Buck is a dog who loves living the outdoor life. He doesn't think much of the other dogs, who live indoors or in the kennels. He is appreciated by the family that owns the land because he is strong and powerful, yet kind.	RL.4.3
	21	B	W.4.5
	22	D	W.4.5
	23	A	W.4.5
	24	D	W.4.5
	25	C	W.4.5
	26	Many think that people my age watch too much TV. Though I enjoy many shows myself, I agree that people my age can overdo it sometimes. when you watch a lot of TV, you're missing out on important exercise that will keep you healthy and fit. TV can also hurt your eyes, because they need to look at things from a distance sometimes to strengthen the eye muscles. Everyone likes TV, but if we can cut down on the amount of TV we watch, we'd probably feel better.	W.4.5

MATHEMATICS PRE-TEST

1. What is the value of $\dfrac{6}{5} + \dfrac{8}{5}$?

2. If $702 = 7 \times 100 + 2$, then what is the remainder of $702 \div 7$?

   A. 2   B. 7   C. 100   D. 700

3. Divide: $3,428 \div 5$. Show your work using an area model.

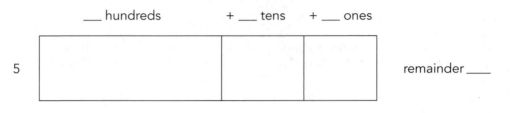

4. Kurt is making a snack mix. He adds $1\dfrac{3}{5}$ cups of cashews and $2\dfrac{3}{5}$ cups of peanuts. How many cups of nuts did he add to the mix?

   A. $3\dfrac{3}{5}$ B. 4 C. $4\dfrac{1}{5}$ D. $5\dfrac{1}{5}$

5. Use $<, >,$ or $=$ to make the number sentence true: $\dfrac{4}{6} \underline{} \dfrac{3}{8}$

6. Which of the following is equivalent to $8 \times \dfrac{5}{2}$?

   A. $\dfrac{13}{2}$ B. $\dfrac{40}{16}$ C. $\dfrac{40}{2}$ D. $\dfrac{13}{10}$

7. Which of the following is equivalent to $5 \times \dfrac{1}{9}$?

   A. $\dfrac{5}{9}$ B. $\dfrac{1}{14}$ C. $\dfrac{6}{9}$ D. $\dfrac{1}{45}$

8. Find the product: $5 \times \dfrac{3}{12}$

9. Biologists monitored the weather of the rainforest during the rainy season. In April, it was sunny on 13 days. On each of the remaining days it rained 3 inches per day. How

many inches of rain fell during April in the rainforest?

10. Each student in a group of 7 students is given $\frac{1}{3}$ cup of sand for a project. In total, how many cups of sand are given to the students?

A. $\frac{8}{3}$ B. $\frac{7}{3}$ C. $\frac{11}{3}$ D. $\frac{10}{3}$

11. Which of the following fractions is equivalent to $\frac{10}{4}$?

A. $\frac{12}{6}$ B. $\frac{8}{2}$ C. $\frac{30}{12}$ D. $\frac{20}{5}$

12. Find the product of 1,208 and 4.

13. Use the area model below to find the product of 42 and 39.

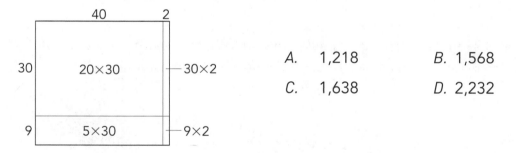

A.   1,218   B. 1,568

C.   1,638   D. 2,232

14. Ms. Lambert's fourth grade class is taking a field trip with Mr. O'Kelly's fifth grade class to the planetarium. There are 23 students in fourth grade and 19 students in fifth grade. The school requires 1 adult chaperone for every 7 students. If Ms. Lambert and Mr. O'Kelly are chaperones, how many more are still needed for the field trip?

A. 4   B. 6   C. 7   D. 8

15. What number in place of the square makes the number sentence true?

A. 3   B. 4   C. 8   D. 10

16. The shelves in Mr. Drake's classroom can each hold 8 books. If he has 70 books, how many shelves will he need to use?

7. Armando wants to use common denominators to compare the fractions below. Which of the following expressions should he use?

$$\frac{3}{4} \underline{\quad} \frac{5}{6}$$

A. $\frac{6}{8} < \frac{5}{8}$

B. $\frac{9}{12} < \frac{10}{12}$

C. $\frac{15}{20} < \frac{15}{18}$

D. $\frac{18}{24} > \frac{20}{24}$

18. Find the sum of $2\frac{1}{8}$ and $7\frac{1}{8}$.

19. Which of the following fractions is equivalent to $\frac{14}{8}$?

A. $\frac{6}{8}$

B. $\frac{7}{4}$

C. $\frac{12}{6}$

D. $\frac{10}{4}$

20. Jerry's family is driving 400 miles to visit his Grandmother. On each of the first two days, they drive 135 miles. How much farther do they have to drive?

21. Which of the following represents the shaded region below?

A. $\frac{5}{8} + \frac{3}{8}$

B. $\frac{4}{5} + \frac{1}{5}$

C. $\frac{2}{8} + \frac{3}{8}$

D. $\frac{3}{5} + \frac{5}{5}$

22. Which of these expressions has the same value as $6,001 \times 4$?

A. $2,400 + 1$ B. $2,400 + 4$ C. $24,000 + 1$ D. $24,000 + 4$

23. Which of the following expressions has the same value as 85×41?

A. $(80+5)+(40+1)$

B. $(80\times5)+(40\times1)$

C. $(80+5)\times(40+1)$

D. $(80\times5)\times(40\times1)$

24. The area of a rectangle is 3,650 square feet. If the width is 5 feet, what is the rectangle's length?

    A. 630   B. 635   C. 730   D. 760

25. Subtract: $4\frac{3}{7} - 2\frac{6}{7}$.

Answer Key

Question	Answer	Explanation	Standard
1	$2\frac{4}{5}$	$\frac{6}{5}+\frac{8}{5}=\frac{6+8}{5}=\frac{14}{5}=\frac{5}{5}+\frac{5}{5}+\frac{4}{5}=1+1+\frac{4}{5}=2\frac{4}{5}$	4.NF.B.3a
2	A	This is the definition of a remainder.	4.NBT.B.6
3	685 R 3	$\underline{6}$ hundreds + $\underline{8}$ tens + $\underline{5}$ ones 5 | 3,000 | 400 | 25 | remainder $\underline{3}$	4.NBT.B.6
4	C	Because adding the two fractional parts will result in an improper fraction, the new fraction must be regrouped into whole numbers. $1\frac{3}{5}+2\frac{3}{5}=1+2+\frac{3}{5}+\frac{3}{5}=3\frac{6}{5}=3+\frac{5}{5}+\frac{1}{5}=4\frac{1}{5}$	4.NF.B.3c, 4.NF.B.3d
5	$\frac{4}{6}>\frac{3}{8}$	Comparing both fractions to $\frac{1}{2}$, $\frac{4}{6}$ is larger since $\frac{3}{6}=\frac{1}{2}$ and $\frac{3}{8}$ is smaller since $\frac{4}{8}=\frac{1}{2}$.	4.NF.A.2
6	C	$8\times\frac{5}{2}=\frac{8\times5}{2}=\frac{40}{2}$	4.NF.B.4, 4.NF.B.4b
7	A	$5\times\frac{1}{9}=\frac{5\times1}{9}=\frac{5}{9}$	4.NF.B.4, 4.NF.B.4a
8	$\frac{15}{12}$	$5\times\frac{3}{12}=\frac{15}{12}$	4.NF.B.4b
9	51 inches	There are 30 days in April, so there were $30-13=17$ days with rain, so it rained $17\times3=51$ inches in April.	4.OA.A.3, 4.NBT.B.5

Question	Answer	Explanation	Standard
10	B	$7 \times \dfrac{1}{3} = \dfrac{7 \times 1}{3} = \dfrac{7}{3}$	4.NF.B.4, 4.NF.B.4b, 4.NF.B.4c
11	C	Multiplying the numerator and the denominator by the same value results in an equivalent fraction. Here the numerator and denominator were both multiplied by 3.	4.NF.A.1
12	4,832	$1{,}208 \times 4 = 4832$	4.NBT.B.5
13	C	Add each area of the rectangle together to find the product of 42 and 39. Because $30 \times 40 = 1{,}200 + 9 \times 40 = 360 + 30 \times 2 = 60 + 9 \times 2 = 18 = 1{,}638$.	4.NBT.B.5
14	A	First, calculate the total number of students going on the field trip: $23 + 19 = 42$. Now, divide that by the number of students for which the school requires 1 chaperone, 7: $42 \div 7 = 6$. Finally, because the 2 teachers are chaperones, subtract 2 from the total needed: $6 - 2 = 4$ more chaperones are needed for the field trip.	4.OA.A.3
15	A	$\dfrac{11}{12} - \dfrac{3}{12} = \dfrac{8}{12}$	4.NF.B.3a, 4.NF.B.3b
16	9	$70 \div 8 = 8$ R 6, therefore he will need 9 shelves	4.NBT.B.6
17	B	The first multiple that 4 and 6 have in common is 12. Because $\dfrac{3}{4} \times \dfrac{3}{3} = \dfrac{9}{12}$ and $\dfrac{5}{6} \times \dfrac{2}{2} = \dfrac{10}{12}$ and $9 < 10$, Armando should use the expression $\dfrac{9}{12} < \dfrac{10}{12}$.	4.NF.A.2, 4.NF.A.1
18	$9\dfrac{2}{8}$	$2\dfrac{1}{8} + 7\dfrac{1}{8} = 9\dfrac{1+1}{8} = 9\dfrac{2}{8}$	4.NF.B.3c
19	B	If the numerator and denominator of $\dfrac{14}{8}$ are both divided by 2, the result is $\dfrac{7}{4}$.	4.NF.A.1
20	130	$400 - 2 \times 135 = 400 - 270 = 130$	4.OA.A.3, 4.NBT.B.5
21	C	The shaded region represents $\dfrac{5}{8}$ and only C shows a sum equivalent to $\dfrac{5}{8}$.	4.NF.B.3a, 4.NF.B.3b
22	D	$6{,}000 \times 4 = (6{,}000 + 1) \times 4 = 6{,}000 \times 4 + 1 \times 4 = 24{,}000 + 4$	4.NBT.B.5, 4.NBT.A.1
23	C	$(80 + 5) \times (40 + 1) = (85) + (41) = 85 + 41$	4.NBT.B.5
24	C	$3{,}650 \div 5 = 730$	4.NBT.B.6
25	$1\dfrac{4}{7}$	Because the fractional part of the second number is greater than the fractional part of the first number, one of the wholes of the first number must be regrouped into a fraction.	4.NF.B.3c

OVERVIEW

For Grade 4, the ELA Common Core Standards focus on main ideas and how they are presented. For informational texts, this means identifying the main idea contained in the passage. The standards also require students to identify and analyze arguments, looking at the reasons and evidence presented by the author. For literary passages, students are expected to be able to identify the theme, and to identify and describe story elements such as character, setting, and events. For writing, students are expected to write opinion pieces that make effective use of arguments, and to use planning and revising to help create stronger writing.

Listed below are the ELA Common Core Standards for Grade 4 that we have identified as "power standards." We consider these standards to be critical for the success for your child. Each lesson in this section focuses on a single power standard so that you and your child may practice that standard to achieve mastery. The applicable standards are divided into three categories: Reading—Informational Text; Reading—Literature; and Writing.

Reading—Informational Text

CCSS.ELA-Literacy.RI.4.1: Refer to details and examples in a text when explaining what the text says explicitly and when drawing inferences from the text.

CCSS.ELA-Literacy.RI.4.2: Determine the main idea of a text and explain how it is supported by key details; summarize the text.

CCSS.ELA-Literacy.RI.4.4: Determine the meaning of general academic and domain-specific words or phrases in a text relevant to a *grade 4 topic or subject area*.

CCSS.ELA-Literacy.RI.4.8: Explain how an author uses reasons and evidence to support particular points in a text.

Reading—Literature

CCSS.ELA-Literacy.RL.4.1: Refer to details and examples in a text when explaining what the text says explicitly and when drawing inferences from the text.

CCSS.ELA-Literacy.RL.4.2: Determine a theme of a story, drama, or poem from details in the text; summarize the text.

CCSS.ELA-Literacy.RL.4.3: Describe in depth a character, setting, or event in a story or drama, drawing on specific details in the text (e.g., a character's thoughts, words, or actions).

CCSS.ELA-Literacy.RL.4.4: Determine the meaning of words and phrases as they are used in a text, including those that allude to significant characters found in mythology (e.g., Herculean).

Writing

CCSS.ELA-Literacy.W.4.1: Write opinion pieces on topics or texts, supporting a point of view with reasons and information.

CCSS.ELA-Literacy.W.4.5: With guidance and support from peers and adults, develop and strengthen writing as needed by planning, revising, and editing.

READING

For the reading standards, Common Core breaks texts into two basic types: (1) Informational Texts, which essentially cover all types of nonfiction; and (2) Literature, which includes stories, drama, and poetry. The following chart from the Common Core Standards Initiative Web site provides a brief overview of the range of text types. For the purposes of assessment, texts are also selected from a broad range of cultures and time periods.

Literature			Informational Text
Stories	Dramas	Poetry	Literary Nonfiction and Historical, Scientific, and Technical Texts
Includes children's adventure stories, folktales, legends, fables, fantasy, realistic fiction, and myth	Includes staged dialogue and brief familiar scenes	Includes nursery rhymes and the subgenres of the narrative poem, limerick, and free verse poem	Includes biographies and autobiographies; books about history, social studies, science, and the arts; technical texts, including directions, forms, and information displayed in graphs, charts, or maps; and digital sources on a range of topics

As practice is the best way to build reading skills, encourage your child to read a variety of literary works and informational texts.

Informational Text

Informational texts include literary nonfiction, such as biographies or memoirs, as well as historical, scientific, and technical texts. They include expository, persuasive, and functional texts in the form of personal essays, opinion pieces, speeches, essays, journalism, and other nonfiction accounts. A variety of types of informational texts is included in this section to give your child practice across a range of genres and subgenres.

Literature

The literature category for grades K-5 includes three main subcategories: stories, dramas, and poetry. Stories may be adventure stories, realistic fiction, folktales and fables, legends and myths, and fantasy. Dramas include the written text that would be used for a play, with dialogue, stage directions, and scenes. Poetry includes nursery rhymes, narrative poems, limericks, and free verse. A variety of stories is included in this section of the book to give your child practice with the genre used most commonly on tests. Because practice is the best way to build reading skills, encourage your child to read a variety of literary works.

WRITING

The Common Core Standards for writing are tied closely to reading. Many of the skills your child learns to read effectively are also applicable to their own writing. In general, your child will be asked to write short passages that express a specific viewpoint or support a specific argument. For these writing passages, the emphasis will be on using information, details, and examples to support the main idea or ideas. Your child will also be expected to create writing that flows smoothly, with an introductory sentence or paragraph, a main body, and a closing sentence or paragraph. In addition to writing an effective draft, your child will also be asked to revise, adjust, and improve their own writing and the writing of others.

Another critical element is mastery of basic grammar and mechanics appropriate for his or her grade level. This is shown through your child's own writing, as well as through revising and improving the writing of others.

THE STANDARD

RI.4.1: *Supporting Evidence and Inferences – Informational Text*
Refer to details and examples in a text when explaining what the text says explicitly and when drawing inferences from the text.

What does it mean?

This informational text standard focuses on a child's ability to recognize how details and examples can be used to explain a text.

Try this together

Here's a brief biography about John Muir that is similar to the kinds of passages used to test this standard. To address this reading standard, a teacher might ask questions such as the ones that follow the passage, or assign them as homework. We have provided possible answers in the "Answers" section, along with an explanation of how the questions connect to the standard.

Before trying this exercise with your child, read through the passage and the questions that follow it yourself. Then have your child read the passage aloud to you and answer the questions that follow. Talk about the answers together. Help your child notice how she can find answers to questions by looking back at the passage.

 ## John Muir

John Muir is one of the most important figures in the establishment of the U.S. national park system. Born in Scotland in 1838, Muir was one of eight children. He and his family moved to the United States when he was just eleven years old. They settled on a farm in Wisconsin, where Muir explored the unspoiled forests and fields around him with his brother. Their father was strict, however, so Muir had to spend much of his childhood studying religious writings instead of observing nature.

Muir's interest in studying nature resurfaced when he was in college in Madison. During his time as a student there, he learned about plants and geology. Even though he was interested in the natural sciences, he spent several years working at sawmills to earn a living. After a factory accident nearly left him blind, Muir decided that he would rather spend his life exploring and documenting nature.

In 1868, Muir traveled to California and settled in the Yosemite Valley. The area featured dramatic peaks and waterfalls, as well as tall redwood trees known as giant sequoias. Muir fell in love with Yosemite, and fought for decades to protect the region from overgrazing and development. He wrote many books and articles about the plant life and geology of Yosemite. These writings captured the imagination of readers around the world and inspired people to look at nature as something worth preserving. He also wrote articles arguing that Yosemite should be protected as a national park. These earned him attention from authors such as Ralph Waldo Emerson, and from politicians like President Theodore Roosevelt. Muir personally appealed to Roosevelt to offer federal protection of Yosemite.

Muir also helped form the Sierra Club in 1892. The Sierra Club had the goal of protecting areas of natural beauty, such as Yosemite. The Sierra Club was instrumental in getting Yosemite and other regions designated as national parks. Muir served as president of the Sierra Club for over twenty years. Even today, the organization continues its quest to preserve natural beauty and a clean environment in the United States, and has over one million members. Largely through the efforts of Muir and other conservationists, the United States created the National Park Service in 1916. Currently, the National Park Service manages over 80 million acres of land, including Yosemite National Park.

❓ Questions

1. Which detail from the first paragraph best sums up how Muir first became interested in nature?

_____

_____

2. What incident made Muir decide to spend his life studying nature?

_____

3. According to the passage, what was it about Yosemite that attracted Muir?

_____

_____

4. Provide at least one example of how Muir fought to protect Yosemite.

_____

_____

5. How did Muir's lifelong efforts contribute to the current U.S. National Park Service? Use details from the passage to support your answer.

_____

_____

 Answers

1. Which detail from the first paragraph best sums up how Muir first became interested in nature? *"They settled on a farm in Wisconsin, where Muir explored the unspoiled*

forests and fields around him with his brother." *This question requires your child to refer to an explicit detail in the text.*

2. What incident made Muir decide to spend his life studying nature? *The factory accident that nearly left Muir blind. This question asks students to recall a specific detail in the passage.*

3. According to the passage, what was it about Yosemite that attracted Muir? *Yosemite has dramatic peaks, waterfalls, and tall redwood trees. Also, it may be inferred that the unspoiled land in general appealed to Muir. This question allows students to provide both details and examples from the text, and also to infer Muir's broader reasons for liking Yosemite.*

4. Provide at least one example of how Muir fought to protect Yosemite. *Examples of how Muir fought to protect Yosemite could include the following: he wrote books and articles about Yosemite; he personally appealed to Roosevelt to protect the region; he helped form the Sierra Club. This question requires students to give one or more examples from the text that relate to Muir's mission to preserve Yosemite.*

5. How did Muir's lifelong efforts contribute to the current U.S. National Park Service? Use details from the passage to support your answer. *These details may include: he helped create the Sierra Club, which lobbied for more national parks; he wrote books and articles on nature that inspired people to view nature as something worth preserving; he fought to protect Yosemite, which paved the way for other areas to be protected. This final question requires students to use details to explain what the text reveals about Muir's contributions.*

Extra practice

To help your child work on the skills assessed by this standard, try this activity:

1. Find a library or online resource containing one of John Muir's many autobiographical works. His book-length writings, as well as many of his articles, are available at www.sierraclub.org.

2. Read through a section of one of his books with your child. Ask him or her to identify details in the text that reveal Muir's love of nature.

Through this activity your child will be directly practicing the skills listed in the standard. He or she will identify specific details within the text that convey Muir's commitment to nature.

Quiz

Have your child read the following informational text and answer the questions that follow.

 The Beatles

On February 7, 1964, American music and pop culture changed forever when a popular band from overseas arrived in the United States. John Lennon, Paul McCartney, George Harrison, and Ringo Starr were The Beatles, a rock-and-roll band originally from Liverpool, England.

Two days later, they appeared on *The Ed Sullivan Show* (a popular television show at the time) and sang their song "I Wanna Hold Your Hand." About 73 million people watched The Beatles on television that night. Screaming teenage fans now followed their every move in the U.S. and "Beatlemania" swept the country, with people imitating their haircuts, their clothes, and their music. Even now, more than 50 years later, many Americans remember where they were when The Beatles first came to visit.

Questions

1. In the second paragraph, what detail most clearly suggests that the Beatles were very popular?

   _____

2. Looking at the context in the second paragraph, what does "Beatlemania" mean?

   _____

3. The first sentence mentions that the Beatles came from "overseas." Which detail in the passage tells you specifically where they came from?

   _____

4. Which detail in the second paragraph supports the first sentence (that American music and pop culture were affected by the Beatles)?

   _____

5. What event made the Beatles so popular in the United States?

   _____

Answers

1. In the second paragraph, what detail most clearly suggests that the Beatles were very popular? *Your child should be able to point out the fact from the second paragraph that 73 million people watched The Beatles on television.*

2. Looking at the context in the second paragraph, what does "Beatlemania" mean? *Your child should be able to use the context details of people imitating the Beatles' hair, clothes, and music in the second paragraph.*

3. The first sentence mentions that the Beatles came from "overseas." Which detail in the passage tells you specifically where they came from? *Your child should look at the second sentence of the first paragraph to illustrate where, specifically, the Beatles were from—Liverpool, England.*

4. Which detail in the second paragraph supports the first sentence (that American music and pop culture were affected by the Beatles)? *In the second paragraph, the detail that many people still remember the Beatles' first American appearance illustrates that the band has had a continuing impact on American culture.*

5. What event made the Beatles so popular in the United States? *Your child should be able to infer that the Beatles' appearance on The Ed Sullivan Show, seen by an audience of 73 million people, made the band popular in the U.S.*

THE STANDARD

RI.4.2: *Main Idea and Key Details – Informational Text*
Determine the main idea of a text and explain how it is supported by key details; summarize the text.

What does it mean?

This informational text standard focuses on a child's ability to identify the main idea in a passage and to recognize details that support the main idea.

Try this together

Here's a brief passage that is similar to the kinds of passages used to test this standard. To address this reading standard, a teacher might ask questions such as the ones that follow the passage, or assign them as homework. We have provided possible answers in the "Answers" section, along with an explanation of how the questions connect to the standard.

Before trying this exercise with your child, read through the passage and the questions that follow it yourself. Then have your child read the passage aloud to you and answer the questions that follow. Talk about the answers together. Help your child notice how she can find answers to questions by looking back at the passage.

 ## Water

On Earth, water is everywhere. It covers more than 70 percent of the planet's surface. It is also present in our ice caps, under the soil as groundwater, and as water vapor in clouds. Most people take water for granted. However, that would be a mistake. Water is one of the most unusual and important substances known to humankind.

From a scientific standpoint, water is a very strange substance. It is one of the few substances to appear in three different forms—solid, liquid, and gas—in our environment. Unlike most substances, water actually becomes less dense as it cools. This is why ice floats. Water has a very high boiling point, which is why so much water on Earth is in liquid form. Liquid water also has a very high surface tension. This is why some insects, such as the water strider, can walk on water without breaking through the surface and getting wet.

Water is also able to dissolve more substances than just about any other liquid. Although we usually think of water as stable and harmless, it can break apart molecules and atoms with great speed and effectiveness. This also means that water can be used in an organism to transport dissolved substances around the body. This includes helpful things like vitamins, which are transported to cells, as well as waste products, which are taken from cells and removed from the body.

Because of its unique characteristics, water is considered to be essential for life as we know it. For example, water makes up about two-thirds of an average human's weight. Without access to drinking water, a human would die within days. Water is also critical to the process of photosynthesis in plants. In addition, water plays an important role in regulating heat on our planet and helps distribute nutrients in the soil through rainfall. Water is a key part of the weather system and shapes the land on which we live through erosion and glaciation. In all these ways, water makes possible the many systems that support life on Earth. The next time you pick up a bottle or glass of water to drink, think about all the weird and wonderful qualities that this amazing liquid possesses.

Questions

1. Which sentence in the first paragraph best expresses the main idea of the passage?

   _____

   _____

2. In the second paragraph, find two details that support the idea that water is an unusual substance.

   _____

   _____

   _____

3. In the third paragraph, what characteristic of water serves as the main idea of the paragraph?

   _____

   _____

4. How do the details in the fourth paragraph differ from the details in the second and third paragraphs?

   _____

   _____

   _____

5. In your own words, write a three-sentence summary of the passage.

   _____

   _____

   _____

   _____

✓ Answers

1. Which sentence in the first paragraph best expresses the main idea of the passage? *The main idea of the passage is best expressed by the following sentence from the first paragraph: "Water is one of the most unusual and important substances known to humankind." This question requires students to identify the main idea of the passage, exactly as the standard dictates. Students should know that the main idea in a passage is often located in the very first paragraph.*

2. In the second paragraph, find two details that support the idea that water is an unusual substance. *Any two of the following details would be correct: water appears in our environment as a solid, a liquid, and a gas; water becomes less dense as it cools; water has a very high surface tension; water has a very high boiling point. This question requires students to identify details that support the main idea of the paragraph. There are other details, such as the fact that a water strider can walk on water without getting wet, but these are secondary to the main point of the paragraph.*

3. In the third paragraph, what characteristic of water serves as the main idea of the paragraph? *Water has the ability to dissolve many things. This question requires students to identify the main idea of the paragraph. Students should know that the main idea of a paragraph is generally the thing that connects all the details within that paragraph together. Since all the details in this paragraph relate to water's ability to dissolve substances, this is clearly the main idea of the paragraph.*

4. How do the details in the fourth paragraph differ from the details in the second and third paragraphs? *The details in the second and third paragraph focus on describing the unusual properties of water. The details in the fourth paragraph focus on explaining how these unusual properties are important in maintaining life on Earth. This is a high-level question that requires students to compare the details presented in the different paragraphs, to see how they are different.*

5. In your own words, write a three-sentence summary of the passage. *Answers will vary, but an acceptable answer will include several important points: water is found all around us; water has many unusual characteristics; water plays an important part in many systems that maintain life on Earth. This requires students to summarize the most important ideas in the passage. Be sure to encourage students to use their own words rather than copying phrases or sentences from the passage.*

Extra practice

To help your child work on the skills assessed by this standard, try this activity:

1. Select a short news article from the newspaper or an online source.
2. Read the article aloud with your child.
3. Ask your child to summarize the article in his or her own words, focusing on the most important ideas presented and avoiding minor details.

Through this activity your child will be directly practicing the skills listed in the standard. He or she will read and summarize an informational article using his or her own words.

Quiz

Have your child read the following informational text and answer the questions that follow.

 Ginger

While you may think of ginger mostly as the flavor in some of your favorite cookies, it is also one of the most useful root plants in the world. From cooking to health, you can find it used on nearly every continent.

Ginger has been grown for hundreds of years in Asian countries like India, China, and Indonesia. Ginger first came to North America in Jamaica, where the first ginger was grown and sent to countries in Europe.

Usually, we think of ginger as food—it can be used in savory, spicy, and sweet dishes. Ginger is a root (much like a potato) that can be peeled, chopped, and cooked in many different dishes. It can also be dried into powder and used as a spice. It might also be coated in sugar and turned into candy, or used in baking cakes, cookies, or other sweets.

Ginger is also commonly used as an herb for health. While it is not a medicine, people in many cultures see it as a treatment for colds, flu, and upset stomach. For example, in China some people cook fresh ginger with brown sugar and water to make a drink to treat common colds. In the Philippines, ginger is often used to make cough drops to help sore throats. And in many countries (including the United States), some believe that ginger ale or other forms of ginger may help with stomachaches or motion sickness.

The next time you're enjoying a gingerbread cookie or sipping a ginger ale, you'll know that you're tasting one of the most common flavors in the world.

 Questions

1. Which sentence from the passage best expresses its main idea?

2. What statement is the main idea of the third paragraph?

3. Name two details that show how people around the world use ginger as a health supplement.

4. What is the main idea of the fourth paragraph?

5. In your own words, write a three-sentence summary of the main points in the passage.

✓ Answers

1. Which sentence from the passage best expresses its main idea? *Your child should able to identify part of the very first sentence, "[ginger] is also one of the most useful root plants in the world," as the passage's main idea.*

2. What statement is the main idea of the third paragraph? *Your child should point to "Usually we think of ginger as food—it can be used in savory, spicy, and sweet dishes" as the main idea of the third paragraph.*

3. Name two details that show how people around the world use ginger as a health supplement. *The fourth paragraph includes three different ways that people use ginger for health, so your child should be able to list the uses in China, the Philippines, or the United States.*

4. What is the main idea of the fourth paragraph? *Your child should be able to identify the first sentence, "Ginger is also commonly used as an herb for health" as the main idea in that paragraph.*

5. In your own words, write a three-sentence summary of the main points in the passage. *Every student's answer will vary, but an acceptable answer will include the following points: the fact that ginger is used around the world; an example of ginger's uses as a food; and an example of ginger's uses for health.*

THE STANDARD

RI.4.8: *Analyzing an Argument – Informational Text*
Explain how an author uses reasons and evidence to support particular points in a text.

What does it mean?

This informational text standard focuses on a child's ability to draw connections between the reasons and evidence presented in a passage and the author's argument or viewpoint.

Try this together

Here's a brief passage about dog-friendly parks that presents a specific argument and viewpoint on the issue. To address this reading standard, a teacher might ask questions such as the ones that follow the passage, or assign them as homework. We have provided possible answers in the "Answers" section, along with an explanation of how the questions connect to the standard.

Before trying this exercise with your child, read through the passage and the questions that follow it yourself. Then have your child read the passage aloud to you and answer the questions that follow. Talk about the answers together. Help your child notice how he or she can find answers to questions by looking back at the passage.

 ## Dog-Friendly Parks

There is much debate over the new park that is opening soon in our town. Some people think that the park should be "dog-friendly." This means that the park would allow owners to take the leashes off their dogs and let them run and play without being tied to their owners. I think this is a bad idea.

The biggest problem with allowing dogs off their leashes is that it is dangerous. A dog could decide to bite someone. People who come to the park are not required to prove that their dog is vaccinated before entering the park. If a person gets bitten by a dog that is not vaccinated, that is very bad for both the dog and the person. Also, people from all over the area will probably use the park. Someone from a different town could bring their dog, and if their dog bites someone, they could leave and no one would know who it was. If a person is bitten by a dog and cannot find out the dog's medical history, this can result in a very dangerous situation.

The dogs could also bite each other. Not all dogs are friendly, and if someone brings a mean dog to the park, all the other dogs could get hurt. Even if a dog is nice, it still might not like a dog it does not know. For example, my dog is very friendly with lots of dogs, but if a strange dog walks by our house, he will bark viciously.

Another big problem with making the park dog-friendly is that the park would have to be fenced off. You cannot just let dogs run around the park without a fence. If you did, the dogs would run out into the street and go wherever they felt like going. Putting a fence around the park would make it less pretty and less welcoming to people without dogs. A fence would also be very expensive.

One more reason to not allow dogs loose in the park is because they probably will not behave themselves. Even if they do not bite someone, dogs are very playful and active. What if a group of people is trying to play a game of softball, and a group of dogs runs out onto the field? Or what if a family is trying to have a picnic in the park, with all their food and drinks laid out on the grass? Do you think a bunch of loose dogs is going to just pass by without trying to steal that food? I have a dog, and I guarantee that he would try to eat every bit of that picnic food!

❓ Questions

1. Describe, in one sentence, the argument the author is making in this passage.

   _____

   _____

2. In the second paragraph, what reasons and evidence are presented to support the argument that allowing dogs off their leashes is dangerous?

   _____

   _____

3. In the third paragraph, what detail from the author's own experience is used to support the argument?

   _____

   _____

4. In the fourth paragraph, what reasons does the author give to argue that a fence around the park would be bad?

   _____

   _____

5. In the fifth paragraph, how does the author use possible situations to illustrate the potential problems with a dog-friendly park?

   _____

   _____

✓ Answers

1. Describe, in one sentence, the argument the author is making in this passage. *Answers will vary, but should contain some of the same basic elements as this example: "The author thinks that having a dog-friendly park is a bad idea." This question requires students to identify the overall point of the passage by looking at the evidence and reasons that are presented.*

2. In the second paragraph, what reasons and evidence are presented to support the argument that allowing dogs off their leashes is dangerous? *Reasons and evidence that support the argument include: dogs could bite someone; owners are not required to prove their dogs have been vaccinated; owners could leave without anyone being able to track them down. This question requires students to recognize specific evidence and reasons for one particular argument within the passage.*

3. In the third paragraph, what detail from the author's own experience is used to support the argument? *The author states that his or her dog is generally friendly but can be aggressive toward dogs it does not know. This question requires students to find a particular type of evidence that is used by the author.*

4. In the fourth paragraph, what reasons does the author give to argue that a fence around the park would be bad? *The student should be able to identify the following reasons: a fence would make the park less appealing to people without dogs; and a fence would be expensive to build. This is another question that asks students to find reasons given by the author in support of a specific argument.*

5. In the fifth paragraph, how does the author use possible situations to illustrate the potential problems with a dog-friendly park? *The student should be able to explain the two "what-if" scenarios the author offers: What if dogs interfere with sporting events? And what if dogs disrupt picnic-goers? This question focuses on one specific type of argument and asks students to explain how the author uses it.*

Extra practice

To help your child work on the skills assessed by this standard, try this activity:

1. Using the Internet, locate a review of a book, movie, or television show that your child is familiar with.

2. Read the review aloud. Then ask your child to explain the reviewer's opinion using his or her own words. Also ask your child to find reasons and examples in the review that support the reviewer's opinion.

3. Ask your child to write his or her own review of the same work. Make sure your child includes reasons and examples to support his or her opinion.

Through this activity, your child will be directly practicing the skills listed in the standard. He or she will examine a written work that expresses a certain opinion or viewpoint and will identify reasons and examples that the author uses to support that opinion.

? Quiz

Have your child read the following argument and answer the questions that follow.

(READ) Biking

Biking is a benefit to any community. It's good for the environment and is a great way to exercise. Our town should create bike lanes downtown so that bicycle riders can travel safely to work, home, and anywhere else they need to go.

Having bike lanes would help the local economy. Gas for cars can be very expensive. If more people were able to bike instead of drive places around town, they would save money on gas and car repairs. It would also save the town money, because fewer cars on the road means spending less money to fix up those roads!

Making it easier to bike instead of drive would also help the environment. Cars and trucks create air pollution. Also, the gas we put in our cars comes from oil, which is a fossil fuel we need to conserve. Biking lets people help limit the fuel they use, which will help make our environmental "footprint" smaller. Anything that helps us be more "green" is a good thing!

Most importantly, creating special lanes for bikes would also make us safer. Traffic can be very dangerous for anyone on a bike—no matter how careful you are, accidents can happen when car drivers don't give bike riders enough space or pay attention to the bike riders around them. Last year, 12 bicycle riders were hurt in road accidents downtown. If bicyclists have their own lanes, it will be easier and safer for them to move along with traffic without being in anyone's way.

? Questions

1. Describe, in one sentence, the main argument the author is making in this passage.

   _____

   _____

2. In the second paragraph, what details does the author use to support the main idea?

   _____

   _____

3. In the third paragraph, what is the author's supporting argument for bike lanes?

   _____

   _____

4. In the fourth paragraph, what specific evidence does the author use to back up his or her main point?

   _____

   _____

5. Which of the author's arguments is presented as the strongest reason to make bike lanes in town?

_____

_____

✓ Answers

1. Describe, in one sentence, the main argument the author is making in this passage. *Your child should be able to identify the third sentence in the first paragraph: "Our town should create bike lanes downtown..."*

2. In the second paragraph, what details does the author use to support the main idea? *Your child should note that gas is expensive, that car and road repairs are expensive, and that drivers and the town can save money by creating bike lanes.*

3. In the third paragraph, what is the author's supporting argument for bike lanes? *The author tells us that bikes are better for the environment, so your child should be able to summarize that briefly.*

4. In the fourth paragraph, what specific evidence does the author use to back up his or her main point? *Your child should point to the specific statistic (Last year, 12 bicycle riders were hurt in road accidents downtown) as evidence for the argument.*

5. Which of the author's arguments is presented as the strongest reason to make bike lanes in town? *"Most importantly" should tell your child that the author is giving extra weight to that particular argument.*

THE STANDARD

RI.4.4: *Vocabulary – Informational Text*
Determine the meaning of general academic and domain-specific words or phrases in a text relevant to a grade 4 topic or subject area.

What does it mean?

This informational text standard focuses on a child's ability to determine the meanings of words by finding clues in the surrounding words and sentences.

Try this together

Here's a brief passage about the rules for a school pool. To address this learning standard, a teacher might ask questions such as the ones that follow the passage, or assign them as homework. We have provided possible answers in the "Answers" section, along with an explanation of how the questions connect to the standard.

Before trying this exercise with your child, read through the passages and the questions that follow it yourself. Then have your child read the passage aloud to you and the answer the questions that follow. Talk about the answers together. Help your child notice how she can find answers to questions by looking back at the passage.

 Pool Rules

The school pool is a place for enjoyment for all students. However, it is essential to remember the safety guidelines so that everyone can have a happy experience.

First, remember that the south end of the pool is too shallow for diving. If you wish to dive, please use only the north end of the pool, which is much deeper.

Second, please remove any loose items such as bracelets, watches, or jewelry before entering the pool. Approximately fifty items are lost annually by students while swimming in the pool, and these items often get stuck in the pool's filter system.

Third, during swim meets, remember to remain within the parallel swim lanes set up by the meet officials. If you swim out of your lane, you might end up hitting another swimmer.

Fourth, please do not bounce repeatedly on the diving board. You may bounce one time when diving. Repeated bouncing causes unnecessary wear and tear on the board.

? Questions

1. Based on its usage in the first paragraph, which of the following is closest in meaning to the word "essential"?

   A. smart   B. required   C. courteous   D. fun

2. Based on its usage in the second paragraph, which of the following is closest in meaning to the word "shallow"?

   A. not well-lit   B. not allowed   C. not serious   D. not deep

3. Based on its usage in the third paragraph, which of the following is closest in meaning to the word "annually"?

   A. every year   B. in the alley
   C. without a problem   D. almost

4. Based on its usage in the fourth paragraph, which of the following is closest in meaning to the word "parallel"?

   A. unable to be crossed
   B. curved and overlapping
   C. straight and in the same direction
   D. invisible

5. Based on its usage in the fifth paragraph, which of the following is closest in meaning to the word "unnecessary"?

   A. relatively tiny   B. not needed   C. over and over   D. not safe

✓ Answers

1. Based on its usage in the first paragraph, which of the following is closest in meaning to the word "essential"? *The correct answer is B. In this passage, "essential" has the same meaning as "required." All questions in this lesson require students to use context and details to determine the meaning of certain words, as dictated by the standard.*

2. Based on its usage in the second paragraph, which of the following is closest in meaning to the word "shallow"? *The correct answer is D. In this passage, "shallow" has the same meaning as "not deep." All questions in this lesson require students to use context and details to determine the meaning of certain words, as dictated by the standard.*

3. Based on its usage in the third paragraph, which of the following is closest in meaning to the word "annually"? *The correct answer is A. In this passage, "annually" has the same meaning as "every year." All questions in this lesson require students to use context and details to determine the meaning of certain words, as dictated by the standard.*

4. Based on its usage in the fourth paragraph, which of the following is closest in meaning to the word "parallel"? *The correct answer is C. In this passage, "parallel" has the same meaning as "straight and in the same direction." All questions in this lesson require students to use context and details to determine the meaning of certain words, as dictated by the standard.*

5. Based on its usage in the fifth paragraph, which of the following is closest in meaning to the word "unnecessary"? *The correct answer is B. In this passage, "unnecessary" has the same meaning as "not needed." All questions in this lesson require students to use context and details to determine the meaning of certain words, as dictated by the standard.*

Extra practice

To help your child work on the skills assessed by this standard, try this activity:

1. Find an encyclopedia and have your child open it to a random page. (This can also be done by viewing an online encyclopedia such as Wikipedia, and randomly clicking one of the many links on the main page.)

2. Then read through the entry you've chosen, and ask your child to point out any unfamiliar words. For each word, prompt your child to use context clues to try to determine the meaning of the word. (Even if your child cannot determine the exact meaning, she may be able to figure out that the word is a noun, for example.)

3. Look up the definitions for all unfamiliar words. Ask your child to make a list of all the new words you encountered, along with their definitions.

Through this activity your child will be directly practicing the skills listed in the standard. He or she will encounter unfamiliar words and attempt to figure out what they mean by using clues in the surrounding text. In addition, your child will expand his or her vocabulary by encountering and defining new words.

Quiz

Have your child read the following text and answer the vocabulary questions that follow.

 Museum Trip

This summer, my family and I visited the National Air and Space Museum in Washington, DC. It was a great trip, and I learned so much about our history in the sky (and in space!).

My favorite exhibit was the one about the Apollo 11 moon landing. The museum had all sorts of **artifacts** from that space mission, like the space suits worn by the astronauts, the maps they made of the **lunar** surface, and even pieces of the moon itself. We even got to see what kind of meals the astronauts had to eat while they were in space. The dried food did not look **appetizing** to me, but it was cool to see what they ate. We also got to watch videos of Neil Armstrong and Buzz Aldrin walking on the moon, and see a life-size **replica** of the lunar lander.

My sister's favorite exhibit taught us about America's **aviation** history, and famous pilots. Did you know that Amelia Earhart was the first woman to fly across the Atlantic Ocean by herself? Or that Orville and Wilbur Wright were the first people to build an airplane that could truly fly? Their "flying machine" only went 120 feet in its first flight, but they helped make today's **aircraft** possible.

? Questions

1. In the second paragraph, which details suggest the meaning of "artifacts"?

   _____

   _____

2. Based on what you know about the passage, what does "aviation" likely mean?

   _____

   _____

3. In the second paragraph, what is the most likely definition of "lunar"?

   _____

   _____

4. Which phrase can help you figure out what the word "appetizing" means: "dried food," "videos of Neil Armstrong and Buzz Aldrin," or "pieces of the moon"?

   _____

   _____

5. Which of the following is closest in meaning to "replica": "replacement," "copy," or "description"?

   _____

   _____

✓ Answers

1. In the second paragraph, which details suggest the meaning of "artifacts"? *Because the writer goes on to list space suits, maps, and pieces of the moon, your child should be able to infer that "artifacts" most likely means "objects."*

2. Based on what you know about the passage, what does "aviation" likely mean? *The main theme of the passage is air and space history, so your student should be able to use that context to figure out that "aviation" history is close to "air" or "flying" history.*

3. In the second paragraph, what is the most likely definition of "lunar"? *Given that the second paragraph is about the moon landing exhibit, your child should make the connection that a "lunar" lander is a "moon" lander.*

4. Which phrase can help you figure out what the word "appetizing" means: "dried food," "videos of Neil Armstrong and Buzz Aldrin," or "pieces of the moon"? *Your child should look at the same sentence as "appetizing" for the direct clue. "Appetizing" comes right after "dried food," so your child should infer that the two are connected and it describes the food directly.*

5. Which of the following is closest in meaning to "replica": "replacement," "copy," or "description"? *The phrase "life-size" should tell your child that "copy" is the closest meaning for "replica."*

THE STANDARD

RL.4.1: *Supporting Evidence and Inferences – Literature*
Refer to details and examples in a text when explaining what the text says explicitly and when drawing inferences from the text.

What does it mean?

This literature standard focuses on a child's ability to recognize how details and examples in a story can be used to explain what the story says.

Try this together

Here's a brief story about a boy who meets a very unusual girl. To address this reading standard, a teacher might ask questions such as the ones that follow the story, or assign them as homework. We have provided possible answers in the "Answers" section, along with an explanation of how the questions connect to the standard.

Before trying this exercise with your child, read through the story and the questions that follow it yourself. Then have your child read the story aloud to you and answer the questions that follow. Talk about the answers together. Help your child notice how she can find answers to questions by looking back at the story.

 Out of the Sky

Cyrus had a knack for being around when weird things happened. There was the time a fire sprinkler went off in Ms. Downworth's class, and it happened to be the one directly over Cyrus's desk. Then there was the time a squirrel followed him all the way home, and then sat outside his bedroom window chattering for two whole hours. And who could forget when Cyrus found a wristwatch in his bowl of chowder at the seafood restaurant downtown?

But the weirdest thing Cyrus ever saw was when he was walking home from school, and—right in front of him—a girl fell out of a tree. She landed flat on her back, and Cyrus thought for a second that she might be dead. But then she moaned, and rolled over onto her side.

Cyrus dropped his backpack and ran to her. "Are you okay?" he asked. He didn't recognize her, so it wasn't likely she lived in the neighborhood.

"Why do you care?" she said, brushing the dirt and leaves from her arms. Cyrus noticed that she was wearing rubber boots that were much too big for her feet. She also wore a white lab coat that looked like a hand-me-down, and glasses that were held together on each side by duct tape. Next to her on the ground was a clipboard covered in scribbled numbers. As soon as she spotted it, she quickly picked it up, pulled a pen from her coat pocket, and started writing.

"I just thought you might need help," said Cyrus.

She looked up, startled, as if she had forgotten he was there. "Help? I don't need anybody's help."

"Really? Do you fall out of trees all the time?"

"I didn't fall out of a tree," she said.

"Yes you did. I saw it."

She shook her head. "I fell out of the sky," she said. "I just passed through the tree on my way down."

"How does somebody fall out of the sky?"

"It's pretty easy. Gravity does most of the work."

"But how did you get up there?"

"Wouldn't you like to know," she replied. Suddenly she stopped scribbling and looked around. "What town is this?" she asked.

Cyrus wasn't sure if she was serious. "Watsonville," he told her.

"Oh," she said, nodding. But then she frowned and fell silent. After an awkward moment, she asked, "Um... what state am I in?"

❓ Questions

1. Give an example of how Cyrus often seems to be present when weird things happen.

   _____

   _____

2. What details does the author use to indicate that Cyrus is a student?

   _____

   _____

3. What details about the girl's appearance seem out of the ordinary?

   _____

   _____

4. Based on the story, would you describe the girl as friendly? Provide details to support your statement.

   _____

   _____

5. Based on the girl's questions at the end of the story, what might you infer about where she is from?

   _____

   _____

✓ Answers

1. *Give an example of how Cyrus often seems to be present when weird things happen.* Any of the following examples would be correct: the fire sprinkler went off above his desk in Ms. Downworth's class; a squirrel followed him home and chattered outside his window; he found a wristwatch in his chowder at a seafood restaurant; and he saw a girl fall out of a tree right in front of him. This question requires students to find examples from the story that support the first sentence. Recognizing examples is key to meeting this standard.

2. *What details does the author use to indicate that Cyrus is a student?* The main detail to indicate that Cyrus is a student is in the second paragraph, where the author states that he was walking home from school. The author also mentions an event that happened in Ms. Downworth's class, suggesting that Cyrus is a student, and further mentions that Cyrus is carrying a backpack. This question requires students to identify details in the story, and to understand how those details inform what the author is saying.

3. *What details about the girl's appearance seem out of the ordinary?* Several details about the girl's appearance seem out of the ordinary: she is wearing very large rubber boots; she is wearing an old lab coat; and she has glasses that are held together with duct tape. Again, this question requires students to identify details that serve a specific purpose.

4. *Based on the story, would you describe the girl as friendly? Provide details to support your statement.* Based on the passage, the girl does not seem friendly. She rejects Cyrus's offer of help and responds rudely to his questions. This question requires students to find details that serve a specific purpose, and also understand how the author uses details to portray a character.

5. *Based on the girl's questions at the end of the story, what might you infer about where she is from?* Answers will vary. Accept any answer that is supported by details in the story. Some students might state that the girl is not from Watsonville, and may be from another state. Some students may infer that she "fell from the sky" because she's from another planet. (The story presents a somewhat unreal situation, so this answer might be given.) This question requires students to make inferences based on details in the story.

Extra practice

To help your child work on the skills assessed by this standard, try this activity:

GO THE EXTRA MILE

1. Ask your child to consider this statement: "Yesterday was the craziest day of my life!"

2. Then ask your child to imagine that this statement is true. How was it crazy? What strange things might have happened? Ask your child to think of four

different examples that show just how crazy yesterday was.

3. Ask your child to write a brief story that begins with the sentence, "Yesterday was the craziest day of my life!" Make sure he or she includes all four examples.

Through this activity, your child will be directly practicing the skills listed in the standard. He or she will identify how details can be used to support ideas in a story.

Quiz

Have your child read the following literature piece and answer the questions that follow.

The Big Game

The big game was scheduled for Saturday, the last weekend before school started for the year. The tournament had been raging all summer, with the neighborhood kids deeply divided. Would the King Street Tigers take the trophy again this year for the third time in a row? Or would the Maple Drive Pirates be able to win it all? The prize was no joke: neighborhood bragging rights all fall and winter long.

The teams had played 10 games this summer, though they'd had to cancel two games due to rain. The Tigers had won five games, and the Pirates had won five. So it all came down to Saturday, and Alex was nervous. She loved playing kickball for the Pirates all summer, but she worried that her fielding skills weren't as good as her kicking. She was a little afraid of what would happen if the ball was kicked right at her during the big game—what if she couldn't get the ball to her teammates in time to make an essential out?

Saturday morning came, and Alex headed to the field along with her teammates, neighbors, and various little brothers, sisters, and friends who were there to watch the last kickball game. Alex was still nervous, but she felt ready.

The Tigers took an early lead, 2-1 going into the last inning. Alex was tense and waited to catch whatever flew her way, but no ball ever came. In their last at-bat inning, her teammate Jenna kicked the ball hard and far, which let her Roger and Angela score. The score was now 3-2, Pirates! Alex walked up to the plate, ready to make their lead even bigger.

The pitcher lobbed the ball at Alex. She was ready for it, and she kicked it with all her might. It was high! It was far! It was...caught, by Jimmy out in the field. Their last at-bat was over, and now the Tigers had the chance to retake the lead.

Disappointed, Alex took her spot back in the field.

"What if they come back and win?" Alex thought. "My team will be so disappointed. We came so close!"

She watched as two Tigers were tagged out on easy infield ground balls. Alex started to feel better—their lead was only one out away from being a win! However, the nervousness came back as she watched Evan come up to the plate. He was the Tigers' best kicker, and boy, did he look determined. On the first pitch, he kicked the ball squarely with a rubbery thump, and Alex could see it hurtling her way.

"C'mon, Alex!" her teammates screamed.

She ran up to try to see where it would land. The bright August sun was in her eyes, and she had trouble seeing the ball in the glare. At the last possible second, Alex could see it falling right in front of her, and she pushed out with her arms. Before she knew what had happened, she felt the ball land with a thud in her arms. She looked down, as her teammates started cheering. Evan was out!

❓ Questions

1. Why is Alex nervous about Saturday's big kickball game?

   _____

   _____

2. Which details tell you what the weather is on the day of the game?

   _____

   _____

3. Based on the text, how many total games would the neighborhood kids have played this summer if there hadn't been any rain-outs?

   _____

   _____

4. What part of playing kickball does Alex see as her strong point?

   _____

   _____

5. Based on Alex catching the ball in the last paragraph, what can you infer about the outcome of the game?

   _____

   _____

✓ Answers

1. Why is Alex nervous about Saturday's big kickball game? *Your child should be able to identify the second paragraph, where the author mentions that Alex is worried about having to field the ball for her team and is scared that she might not be able to catch the ball at a key moment.*

2. Which details tell you what the weather is on the day of the game? *Your child should be able to find the mention of the sun in the last paragraph. Also, it's mentioned in the second paragraph that previous games were cancelled because of rain—so your child can also infer that if the teams were playing, it couldn't have been raining on the Saturday of the last game.*

3. Based on the text, how many total games would the neighborhood kids have played this summer if there hadn't been any rain-outs? *Your child should note that there were 10 games already played before, two games rained out, and one final game, for a total of 13 games.*

4. What part of playing kickball does Alex see as her strong point? *In the second paragraph, Alex worries that her fielding isn't as good as her kicking, so your child should be able to infer that Alex believes she is good at kicking.*

5. Based on Alex catching the ball in the last paragraph, what can you infer about the outcome of the game? *The fourth paragraph tells the reader that this is the last inning and that the Pirates are ahead 3-2. The eighth paragraph tells the reader that the Tigers are down to their last out, so your child should be able to use that information to conclude that the Pirates have won the game.*

THE STANDARD

RL.4.2: *Theme – Literature*
Determine a theme of a story, drama, or poem from details in the text; summarize the text.

What does it mean?

This literature standard focuses on a child's ability to identify the theme, or lesson, of a story, and to provide a summary of it.

Try this together

Here's a brief story that focuses on a specific theme. To address this reading standard, a teacher might ask questions such as the ones that follow the story, or assign them as homework. We have provided possible answers in the "Answers" section, along with an explanation of how the questions connect to the standard.

Before trying this exercise with your child, read through the story and the questions that follow it yourself. Then have your child read the story aloud to you and answer the questions that follow. Talk about the answers together. Help your child notice how she can find answers to questions by looking back at the story.

 On the Moon

Dylan looked out the dining room bay window and sighed. Outside was a vast expanse of gray nothingness under a black sky dotted with stars. And of course there was Earth, blue and green and looking almost close enough to touch. Dylan was the only person on the moon, but that didn't make him feel special. It just made him feel alone. He wondered how many people down there were looking up at him without even realizing it.

He slurped his dinner from a single-serving pouch. "Beef stew," the pouch read. He was pretty sure it didn't taste much like actual beef stew, but it had been so long since he'd tasted real food that he couldn't judge how bad it was. It didn't matter, anyway. Back on Earth, food meant family and friends gathering together, sharing in a lovingly prepared bounty of fresh ingredients. Here, food was just fuel for the engine of his body. He ate simply to keep going.

After dinner, Dylan checked on the processors. They looked like buildings, but with treads on either side, like tanks. Each one scooped up tons of soil, sifted through it for precious metals, and then slowly moved to another spot and did it all again. His job was to make sure the processors kept doing their job. Each processor was temperamental in its own way. Dylan gave them names that matched their personalities. The one that sputtered and shook all the time, as if it were on the verge of giving up entirely, was named Gus. The smallest and newest processor, which moved at twice the speed of the older units, he named Zip. The others were named after people he knew back on Earth—there was Addy, and Herc, and Daphne, and so on. He often talked to them, though they only answered with the same dull drone.

"Way to move, Zip!" he called out as the littlest processor kicked up dust.

Dylan walked over to his main viewscreen and brought up a calendar. He drew an "X" with his finger, marking off another day. "Four thousand, two hundred and sixteen to go," he said to no one, and stared out at the blue-green orb he longed to call home once more.

 Questions

1. How would you describe the theme, or lesson, of this story?

   _____

   _____

2. In three sentences or less, summarize the events that occur in the story.

   _____

   _____

3. How does the author's description of dinner emphasize the theme of the story?

   _____

   _____

4. How does Dylan's attitude toward the processors reflect the theme?

   _____

   _____

5. Based on the details in the story, what real-world job would you say most closely resembles Dylan's job in the story?

   _____

   _____

☑ Answers

1. How would you describe the theme of this story? *Answers will vary. Many students will say that the theme has to do with loneliness—that human contact is key to human happiness. Accept answers that are well-supported by details in the story. This question requires students to identify the theme of the passage, just as the standard dictates. Note that the theme often goes beyond surface details; for example, a student might state that*

the passage is about "space" or "the moon." However, neither of these is the best way of expressing the theme of the story.

2. In three sentences or less, summarize the events that occur in the story. *Answers will vary but should be similar to the following: Dylan lives completely alone on the moon, where he takes care of mining equipment. He eats dinner by himself, talks to the machines he services, and looks forward to the day he can return to Earth. This question requires students to summarize the story, or retell important events that occur in the plot.*

3. How does the author's description of dinner emphasize the theme of the story? *The author describes dinner as something to simply fuel Dylan's body. This is in contrast to the Dylan's thoughts about meals back on Earth, which were filled with companionship and love. The author uses this contrast to emphasize Dylan's loneliness. This question requires students to describe how details within the story relate to the theme.*

4. How does Dylan's attitude toward the processors reflect the theme? *Dylan treats the processors like people because he lacks anyone else to talk to. He not only talks to them; he has named them after people he knows back on Earth. This reflects the loneliness he feels working alone on the moon. This is another question that requires students to describe how details within the story relate to the theme.*

5. Based on the details in the story, what real-world job would you say most closely resembles Dylan's job in the story? *Based on the details provided, Dylan's job closely resembles that of a mechanic. He might also be considered a technician, or even a programmer if the reader assumes that the processors are complex pieces of technology. This question requires students to compare details in the story to real-life jobs they might know something about. Answers will vary but should be well-supported.*

Extra practice

To help your child work on the skills assessed by this standard, try this activity:

1. Ask your child to write a list of things he or she thinks of when hearing the word "friendship."

2. Then ask your child to use that list to write a brief story on the theme of friendship. He or she should try to incorporate as many associations as possible.

3. Read the story aloud and discuss how the different elements of friendship made their way into the story.

Through this activity, your child will be directly practicing the skills listed in the standard. He or she will recognize how a theme is supported by details within the story and will be able to better understand the techniques used by authors when developing themes in literature.

? Quiz

Have your child read the following literature piece and answer the questions that follow.

Phone Quest

Felix had looked everywhere for his cell phone. So far, the search was totally disappointing. The phone wasn't in any of his pant pockets (he'd checked each one at least twice, just to make sure) or his coat pockets. And it definitely wasn't in the car—he spent 20 minutes checking every nook and cranny. He had found $3.26 in loose change, and several wrapped sticks of gum that had fallen under the seat—but no phone. Where could it be?

While he was searching his car, Felix's neighbor had come outside and noticed that Felix was desperately searching for something. When Felix told her that he was hunting for his phone, she made a very smart suggestion.

"Why don't you retrace your steps?" she asked. Of course! Felix remembered that he had gotten a text message from his friend Tom while at the grocery store. Maybe it was there!

Unfortunately, there was no sign of the phone at the grocery store, not in the cereal aisle where he remembered responding to the text message, and not in any of the other aisles either. On to the next place: Felix had visited the bank after he'd bought his groceries.

"Have you seen my phone?" he asked the bank teller at the desk. "It's small and black, and it has a photo of my gray cat on the main screen," he told her.

"I'm sorry, sir, no one has found a phone like that today," she told him regretfully. She wished him luck in his search. The bank was the last place Felix had stopped before he went home, so he was out of options. As he walked back toward the door, discouraged, the bank teller called out to him.

"Have you tried calling your number?" she asked. Felix hadn't, so the teller offered him a phone to use. Felix dialed, and heard his own phone ring twice. Then—a miracle!—a voice answered.

"Hello?"

"Hi! My name is Felix, and I think you've found my phone."

"Oh, that's great," the mysterious voice answered. "I was wondering how to find you after I found your phone at the grocery store."

They made plans for Felix to pick up his lost (and now found!) phone, and a very relieved Felix decided he would be much more careful with his phone the next time he was out running errands.

? Questions

1. In three sentences or less, summarize the events of the story.

   _____

   _____

   _____

   _____

2. What word would you use to describe the theme of the story?

   _____

3. What details does the author use to emphasize the theme of the story?

_____

_____

4. Based on the passage, how do you know Felix is relieved to have his phone back?

_____

_____

5. How does Felix's mood throughout the story emphasize the theme?

_____

_____

_____

 Answers

1. In three sentences or less, summarize the events of the story. *Answers will vary, but your child's answer should include something along the lines of: Felix loses his phone, Felix searches for his phone, and Felix finds his phone.*

2. What word would you use to describe the theme of the story? *Answers will vary, but could include words like "loss," "lost and found," or "searching."*

3. What details does the author use to emphasize the theme of the story? *Your child should be able to identify the different places Felix searches for his phone right when he realizes it's lost, the places he goes when he decides to retrace his steps, or the people he talks to during his search.*

4. Based on the passage, how do you know Felix is relieved to have his phone back? *Your child should be able to differentiate between "discouraged" Felix in the sixth paragraph and the "miracle" of finding it in the seventh paragraph.*

5. How does Felix's mood throughout the story emphasize the theme? *Your child should be able to point to words like "disappointing" and "discouraged" to support the theme of loss.*

THE STANDARD

RL.4.3: *Characters and Story Elements – Literature*
Describe in depth a character, setting, or event in a story or drama, drawing on specific details in the text (e.g., a character's thoughts, words, or actions).

What does it mean?

This literature standard focuses on a child's ability to describe characters, settings, and events in their own words after reading a passage.

Try this together

Here's a brief passage that offers a detailed description of a character and setting. To address this reading standard, a teacher might ask questions such as the ones that follow the passage, or assign them as homework. We have provided possible answers in the "Answers" section, along with an explanation of how the questions connect to the standard.

Before trying this exercise with your child, read through the passage and the questions that follow it yourself. Then have your child read the passage aloud to you and answer the questions that follow. Talk about the answers together. Help your child notice how she can find answers to questions by looking back at the passage.

 ## The Woodsman

Torvald came from the darkest depths of the woods, where even the bears were too nervous to venture. His home was carved out of the belly of a giant redwood tree. It was nothing more than a circular room with a bed and a place for a fire. The outer edge of the massive trunk still stood as a wall, broken only by the small archway he used as a door. If you looked at the floor of the home, you could count the rings and see how many centuries the tree had lived before Torvald claimed it as his own.

The giant redwood stood in a valley so deep that it only saw sunlight for two hours each day. Even then, the sun's rays scarcely made it through the dense forest canopy to reach the ground below. Instead of flowers, the ground was covered with dead leaves, mosses, and mushrooms large enough to sit upon. The only animals that lived in the valley were the king toads, with their thundering croaks and poisonous skin, and the ghost bats, with their glowing eyes and broad leathery wings. And, of course, Torvald.

Torvald himself could easily be mistaken for a tree under the right circumstances. He was built like a stump, solid and impossible to knock down. His arms were sinewy like branches, and were covered with skin as thick and dry as bark. And his hair! It covered his head, face, and chest in a thick dark tangle, and shot through it all were vines and moss that must have been growing for years. Torvald didn't need a shave and a haircut—he need a mowing and a pruning.

If you ran into Torvald in the darkest part of the forest, you would no doubt take him for a troll and run away screaming. In truth, he was the gentlest soul you could hope to meet. If, instead of running away, you offered a friendly greeting, Torvald would let out a bellowing laugh that shook the ground and sent the ghost bats fluttering like a whirlwind. Then he would slap you on the back with his brick-hard hand and invite you back to his house for mushroom tea.

Questions

1. Which story element (character, plot, setting) is the focus of the first two paragraphs of the passage?

2. What words would you use to describe Torvald's appearance?

3. Which specific details in the passage suggest that Torvald is strong?

4. According to the passage, how does Torvald's personality differ from his appearance?

5. How do the details of the setting help create an image of a scary place?

Answers

1. Which story element is the focus of the first two paragraphs of the passage? *The setting is the focus of the first two paragraphs of the passage. This question requires students to recognize the main story element at work in this part of the passage.*

2. What words would you use to describe Torvald's appearance? *Answers will vary but should build upon some of the details found in the passage. Answers might include descriptions such as "tree-like," "frightening," "ugly," "large," "hairy," and "troll-like." This*

question requires students to describe a character using their own words, in line with the spirit of the standard.

3. Which specific details in the passage suggest that Torvald is strong? *There are a number of details in the passage that suggest Torvald is strong. These include descriptions such as "built like a stump," "impossible to knock down," and "brick-hard hand." The reader might also infer that Torvald carved his own home out of a giant tree, a feat which would require great strength. This question requires students to find details regarding the character of Torvald and to determine which of these details is used by the author to convey strength.*

4. According to the passage, how does Torvald's personality differ from his appearance? *Although his appearance is scary, Torvald is a gentle and kind person who enjoys laughing. This question requires students to compare the details of his personality with the details of his appearance.*

5. How do the details of the setting help create an image of a scary place? *The author focuses on the darkness of the valley and mentions plants and animals that are usually considered creepy or gross, such as bats, toads, and mushrooms. This question requires students to find details regarding the setting and to explain how these details convey a scary mood.*

Extra practice

To help your child work on the skills assessed by this standard, try this activity:

1. Ask your child to choose a notable person in his or her life. This should be a person your child knows well and can easily picture in his or her head.

2. Then ask your child to write down a list of details about that person. Be sure your child includes details about the person's appearance, as well as details about the person's personality, speech, and actions.

3. Ask your child to put this detailed character into a silly story of their own creation.

Through this activity, your child will be directly practicing the skills listed in the standard. He or she will learn to recognize the importance of details when describing a person and will be better equipped to understand how authors use these same techniques when developing characters in literary works.

❓ Quiz

Have your child read the following literature piece and answer the questions that follow.

 ## It's a Wash

Carl looked at his workspace with satisfaction. He had everything ready in his backyard: a big plastic tub, a hose, plenty of shampoo, and a pile of fluffy towels. He and his sister Melanie had put up fliers all over the neighborhood telling everyone about their services for noon on Saturday. Now he just needed customers to show up.

Carl didn't have to wait long: his friend Jake showed up at 12:00 on the dot with his bulldog Bones in tow. Finally, Carl's dog washing business was on its way. Bones was a pretty easy customer—he enjoyed the cool water in the tub and he didn't even seem to mind when Carl accidentally got some soap bubbles in his nose. By the time Bones was washed, dried, and on his way, there were two more people on deck, with customers waiting patiently on leashes for their turns.

While Carl washed the dogs, Melanie had put herself in charge of keeping everyone in line, collecting money, and giving biscuits to the clean customers on their way out. While there were some scuffles in line (like when Princess the Chihuahua didn't get along with Marvin the Terrier), things went pretty smoothly overall. She was good at organizing. And although she didn't really like the smell of wet dogs, when she saw that Carl was the one covered with soapy water every time a dog decided to shake his fur while standing in the tub, Melanie figured she had the better end of the deal.

By 2:00, Carl and Melanie had washed six different dogs, including Mrs. Jackson's two hyper border collies from next door and their own golden retriever, Bob. They had even had a surprise customer: Melanie's friend Ashley from down the street had brought a pet carrier, which turned out to hold her cat, Herman. Carl didn't know much about cats, but thanks to the scratches on his arm and Herman's ear-splitting yowls, he knew that cats did not like to be washed.

"At least this will be good practice for the future," thought Carl (who wanted to be a veterinarian someday).

By 3:00, they were done, after the last dog had trotted away with her biscuit and her very pleased owner. At $5 per dog, Carl and Melanie had made $50 (plus a generous $3 tip from Mr. Henderson, whose Labradoodle had jumped out mid-bath and run around the yard until Carl could grab him and get him back into the tub).

"We should do this again next Saturday," Melanie announced happily after they'd counted their profits.

"Sure. I should be just about dried out by then," Carl replied, tired but happy at the success of their new business.

❓ Questions

1. Which story element (character, plot, setting) is the focus of the first paragraph?

   _____

   _____

2. Which story element (character, plot, setting) is the focus of the second paragraph?

3. Which story element (character, plot, setting) is the focus of the third paragraph?

4. From the context of the passage, how does Carl end up with scratches on his arm?

5. Based on what you learn about Carl in the passage, what might be his motivation for choosing dog washing as a business?

 **Answers**

1. Which story element (character, plot, setting) is the focus of the first paragraph? *Because the first paragraph describes Carl's backyard and the objects in it, your child should be able to identify this paragraph as a setting.*

2. Which story element (character, plot, setting) is the focus of the second paragraph? *This paragraph is about the action of Carl and Melanie's dog washing business, so your child should be able to identify this as a plot-focused paragraph.*

3. Which story element (character, plot, setting) is the focus of the third paragraph? *This paragraph is the first one that gives you details on Melanie, so your child should be able to identify this as a character-focused section.*

4. From the context of the passage, how does Carl end up with scratches on his arm? *Your child should be able to infer that the scratches came from Herman, the cat who did not want to be washed.*

5. Based on what you learn about Carl in the passage, what might be his motivation for choosing dog washing as a business? *In paragraph five, the reader learns that Carl wants to be a veterinarian someday, which could explain why he chooses to work with animals for his backyard business.*

THE STANDARD

RL.4.4: Vocabulary – Literature
Determine the meaning of words and phrases as they are used in a text, including those that allude to significant characters found in mythology (e.g., Herculean).

What does it mean?

This literature standard focuses on a child's ability to determine the meanings of words by finding clues in the surrounding words and sentences. In particular, this standard includes vocabulary words derived from characters in mythology.

Try this together

Here's a brief story about two girls and the hat that links them together. To address this reading standard, a teacher might ask questions such as the ones that follow the story, or assign them as homework. We have provided possible answers in the "Answers" section, along with an explanation of how the questions connect to the standard.

Before trying this exercise with your child, read through the story and the questions that follow it yourself. Then have your child read the passage aloud to you and answer the questions that follow. Talk about the answers together. Help your child notice how he or she can find answers to questions by looking back at the story.

 Hat Girl

Exactly two weeks into the new school year, I decided that Lucy Beckwith was my nemesis. A casual observer might say that I had no reason to hate her, and they might be right. She was sweet and kind to just about everyone, including me. Whenever she walked into a room, it suddenly became a little brighter. Her sunny attitude seemed to come from the brightly colored hat she started wearing two weeks into the school year—a floppy bucket hat covered in a flower print. Lots of people just called her "Hat Girl."

Here's the thing: it was my hat. Mom didn't have any right to donate it to the thrift store. She never even asked me if it was okay. I got that hat during our summer trip to the beach house when I was ten. True, I didn't wear it much; it just sat at the bottom of my closet because I was too afraid that someone at school would make fun of it. But still, the first time I saw Lucy wearing my hat... it took a herculean effort to stop myself from yanking it off her head and shouting, "MINE!"

As soon as I decided that Lucy was my sworn enemy, I came up with a plan: I would find out where she lived, and then I would steal my hat back. One day after school, I began my odyssey to reclaim the hat. I followed her from a distance, so she wouldn't see me. She lived very far from the school, in a cramped neighborhood filled with small, lopsided houses that all needed a fresh coat of paint.

I saw her go inside one especially tiny house, and I crept up to her bedroom window. I figured she would leave the hat somewhere in her room, and I could sneak in and take it. Her room was Spartan, with just an empty desk and a neatly made bed. There were no posters on the wall, no television, no dolls or stuffed animals. It was a sad, dark, tiny room.

Suddenly I felt like I had made a colossal mistake. That hat was the one bright, colorful thing Lucy Beckwith had. It gave her a reason to be outgoing and friendly.

That was when I decided that Lucy would not be my nemesis, but my friend. And you know what? That hat looks better on her than it ever did on me.

? Questions

1. Based on its usage in the first paragraph, which of the following is closest in meaning to the word "nemesis"?

   A. mentor   B. enemy   C. friend   D. stranger

2. Based on its usage in the second paragraph, which of the following is closest in meaning to the word "herculean"?

   A. requiring great strength   B. having large muscles
   C. violent   D. without words

3. Based on its usage in the third paragraph, which of the following is closest in meaning to the word "odyssey"?

   A. weird occurrence   B. complaint
   C. hope   D. journey

4. Based on its usage in the fourth paragraph, which of the following is closest in meaning to the word "Spartan"?

   A. without decoration or excess   B. large and spacious
   C. filled with lots of light   D. artistically decorated

5. Based on its usage in the fifth paragraph, which of the following is closest in meaning to the word "colossal"?

   A. cold and brittle   B. unimportant
   C. huge   D. considerate

✓ Answers

1. Based on its usage in the first paragraph, which of the following is closest in meaning to the word "nemesis"? *The correct answer is B. In this passage, "nemesis" has the*

same meaning as "enemy." All questions in this lesson require students to use context and details to determine the meaning of certain words. In Greek mythology, Nemesis was a goddess of vengeance.

2. Based on its usage in the second paragraph, which of the following is closest in meaning to the word "herculean"? *The correct answer is A. In this passage, "herculean" has the same meaning as "requiring great strength." In Roman mythology, Hercules was a demigod of great strength.*

3. Based on its usage in the third paragraph, which of the following is closest in meaning to the word "odyssey"? *The correct answer is D. In this passage, "odyssey" has the same meaning as "journey." In Greek mythology, Odysseus was a man who went on a ten-year journey to return home to his wife.*

4. Based on its usage in the fourth paragraph, which of the following is closest in meaning to the word "Spartan"? *The correct answer is A. In this passage, "Spartan" has the same meaning as "without decoration or excess." In Greek mythology, the Spartans were warriors from the city of Sparta, who lived without anything fancy or excessive.*

5. Based on its usage in the fifth paragraph, which of the following is closest in meaning to the word "colossal"? *The correct answer is C. In this passage, "colossal" has the same meaning as "huge." Colossus was a huge bronze statue located at the island of Rhodes.*

Extra practice

To help your child work on the skills assessed by this standard, try this activity:

1. Help your child recall the definitions of each of these words: *nemesis, herculean, odyssey, Spartan,* and *colossal.*
2. Together, brainstorm situations in which these words might be used.
3. Ask your child to write his or her own story that makes use of these words.

Through this activity, your child will be directly practicing the skills listed in the standard. By becoming familiar with these words, especially those based on characters from mythology, your child will expand his or her vocabulary.

Quiz

Have your child read the following literature piece and answer the questions that follow.

The Election

The election was over, and Margo had lost. It had been a good campaign: she had met with her fellow students, listened to them talk about what they wanted in school, and told them what she would have done if she was named class president. She had made giant, colorful posters and adhered them to walls all around the school. She had given a great speech, talking about changes she felt would make the school better... like a veggie pizza option in the cafeteria on Pizza Friday, more photography classes, and an international fair where students could learn more about world cultures.

However, Amber Jensen had won in the end. Amber had promised the students Taco Thursdays in addition to Pizza Fridays and better equipment for the flag football club that met after school. Plus, Amber seemed to know everyone in the school. It was hard to compete with that. Amber would be their class president, representing the 8th grade class in student government meetings.

In the meantime, the votes had been counted, and it was time for Margo to go home for the day. As she walked out to the parking lot, where her dad was probably already waiting to pick her up, Margo noticed one of her posters still on the wall. "Margo 4 President," it read in big letters.

"Not this year," she said sadly as she gingerly pulled it down, trying not to rip the paper. "But then again—maybe next year!"

Questions

1. In the first paragraph, which of the following is closest in meaning to "campaign": "mission," "contest," or "advertisement"?

   _____

   _____

2. In the first paragraph, which details tell you what "adhered" most likely means?

   _____

   _____

3. Based on its usage in the second paragraph, what do you think is the meaning of "compete"?

   _____

   _____

4. In the fourth paragraph, which of the following is closest in meaning to "gingerly": "roughly," "easily," or "carefully"?

   _____

   _____

5. Which details in the fourth paragraph can tell you what "gingerly" means?

   _____

   _____

✓ Answers

1. In the first paragraph, which of the following is closest in meaning to "campaign": "mission," "contest," or "advertisement"? *Because the author has already told the reader that Margo has lost, your child should infer that "contest" is closer to "campaign" than either of the other options.*

2. In the first paragraph, which details tell you what "adhered" most likely means? *Your child should look at "poster" and "on the wall" to help determine that "adhered" means "stuck," or "hung," or similar.*

3. Based on its usage in the second paragraph, what do you think is the meaning of "compete"? *As in the first paragraph, the discussion of winning and losing should tell your child that to "compete" means to "race," or "have a contest," or similar.*

4. In the fourth paragraph, which of the following is closest in meaning to "gingerly": "roughly," "easily," or "carefully"? *The passage tells the reader that Margo was trying not to rip the paper, so your child should be able to infer that "roughly" and "easily" don't quite fit.*

5. Which details in the fourth paragraph can tell you what "gingerly" means? *Once your child has identified the correct context detail for question 4, he or she should be able to answer this question by pointing to the phrase "trying not to rip the paper."*

THE STANDARD

W.4.1: *Writing Arguments*
Write opinion pieces on topics or texts, supporting a point of view with reasons and information.
- **W.4.1a:** *Introduce a topic or text clearly, state an opinion, and create an organizational structure in which related ideas are grouped to support the writer's purpose.*
- **W.4.1b:** *Provide reasons that are supported by facts and details.*
- **W.4.1c:** *Link opinion and reasons using words and phrases (e.g., for instance, in order to, in addition).*
- **W.3.2d:** *Provide a concluding statement or section related to the opinion presented.*

What does it mean?

This standard focuses on a child's ability to write a well-organized paragraph or series of paragraphs. It is designed to assess how well a child can develop a topic by providing appropriate supporting information and make connections between and among the ideas.

The focus of this writing standard is writing an opinion or argument. Opinion pieces are defined as those in which the writer develops a logical, well-supported argument or claim based on evidence. Sometimes referred to as persuasive writing, these pieces attempt to convince the reader that the ideas and opinions presented are worth adopting.

As shown in the sub-steps of the W.4.1 writing standard, the writing assesses the basic elements of a paragraph or essay, including the introduction (W.4.1a), body (W.4.1.b), and conclusion (W.4.1d). It also focuses on using linking words and phrases to connect ideas.

Try this together

Regardless of their skill level, all writers get better with practice. Unfortunately, many young writers become overwhelmed when writing is taught all at once. It may help to break down the writing process and focus on one part of the W.4.1 standard at a time. We will look at how this might be done.

Here's a writing prompt similar to one that might be used to test this standard. We have provided a sample answer, along with an explanation of how it all connects to the standard.

Prompt

What is your favorite food? And why is it your favorite? Write a paragraph discussing your favorite food and why it is your favorite. Be sure to include facts and details to support your opinion.

After reading the prompt, have your child to write a topic sentence that states the opinion he or she wants to present.

Next, ask your child to think of facts and details that will help convince readers that the chosen favorite food really is great. As your child writes these facts and details into the body of the paragraph, encourage him or her to use words and phrases that connect ideas.

Finally, have your child write a concluding sentence. Explain that the conclusion should sum up the main opinion presented in the paragraph. It should not introduce new ideas.

Sample Answer

My favorite food is pizza. I like pizza for many reasons. First, it combines a lot of other good foods. Pizza has bread on the bottom, sauce in the middle, and cheese on top. Plus you can have all kinds of other good things on top too, like meat or vegetables. Second, I like pizza because you can get it almost anywhere. There are pizza restaurants in just about every town, and you can also buy it frozen at the store. In addition, pizza is my favorite food because it has the best taste of anything ever invented. I love the taste so much that I would eat pizza all the time if my parents would let me. Without a doubt, pizza is the best food ever.

The main goal of this standard is to encourage students to formulate opinions and back them up with facts and details. Note how in the sample answer, the student provides three distinct reasons why pizza is his or her favorite food. These reasons can be subjective, such as the claim that pizza has the best taste of anything ever invented. However, it is important to provide reasons with as much specific detail as possible. Simply stating "Pizza is my favorite because I really like it" would not be sufficient for this standard.

Also note that words and phrases, such as *first*, *second*, and *in addition*, help link the ideas together, and that the concluding sentence restates the main opinion presented in the paragraph.

Extra practice

To help your child work on the skills assessed by this standard, try this activity:

1. Use the following as a writing prompt for a short piece of writing: "What is your favorite animal, and why is it your favorite?"

2. Before your child begins writing, discuss the prompt and have him or her give reasons for their choice of favorite animal. Be sure to ask for specific details that support the reasons given.

3. Encourage your child to make notes of the reasons he or she gave during your discussion. These notes can then be used as the basis for the piece of writing.

4. Remind your child to write a concluding sentence that sums up the main opinion given.

Through this activity, your child will be directly practicing the skills listed in the standard. He or she will present an opinion on a topic and will support that opinion with reasons that are bolstered by specific facts and details.

Quiz

Read each of the following prompts, and then answer the question that follows. (Note that Questions 1-3 do not require an extended writing response.)

1. What is your favorite subject in school, and why? Write a paragraph discussing the school subject you like best. Be sure to discuss examples to support your opinion.

   Which of the following is an example of a good sentence to support your opinion?
   A. *Math is the last subject of the day.*
   B. *I want to be a scientist when I grow up, so I love to see what happens when we do experiments.*
   C. *We have to change clothes for P.E. class, because otherwise our clothes would get dirty.*
   D. *I doodle a lot in my notebook and people say I am good at making bubble letters.*

2. A group of students wants to start a new dance club after school. Students will try out for the club, and only students who the club thinks are good enough will be allowed to join. Do you think it's fair for the school to let the students start this club? Be sure to include reasons and facts to support your choice.

   Which of the following is NOT a strong sentence to support your argument?
   A. *I don't like to dance at all, and I wouldn't be interested in this club.*
   B. *If the tryouts are fair, then there is no reason why this should not be allowed.*
   C. *This club would not take place during school hours, so it seems okay to not let everyone join.*
   D. *Not everyone likes to dance, so it's okay to have a club only for people who want to stay late and dance when school is over.*

3. Some schools have made a rule that teachers are not allowed to use cell phones why they are in the classroom. Do you think this is a fair rule for schools to make? Be sure to discuss examples to support your opinion.

Which of the following is an example of a good sentence to support your opinion?
   A. *Mrs. Deeds has an iPhone and likes to check Facebook.*
   B. *I think students should be allowed to keep a phone in their bag if their parents let them, in case of emergencies.*
   C. *Mrs. Deeds didn't hear me ask her a question the other day because she was checking a text message on her phone.*
   D. *Teachers sometimes leave their phones at home anyway.*

For questions 4 and 5, have your child write a one-paragraph response to the prompts below.

4. What is your favorite sport? And why is it your favorite? Write a paragraph discussing your favorite sport, and why it is your favorite. Be sure to include reasons and facts that support your opinion.

_____

_____

_____

_____

5. Where would you go if you could choose anywhere to travel on a vacation? Write a paragraph discussing to where you would travel, and why. Be sure to include reasons and facts that support your opinion.

_____

_____

_____

_____

☑ Answers

1. Which of the following is an example of a good sentence to support your opinion? *The correct answer is B. This is a strong supporting sentence because it gives a specific reason why the writer likes science class, and how it applies to her life. The other sentences are not as clear and direct as sentence B.*

2. Which of the following is NOT a strong sentence to support your argument? *The correct answer is A. This sentence is a fact that only applies to the writer. It does not support an argument why or why hot he feels this club should be allowed at the school. The other*

three sentence all offer clear supporting evidence why the writer thinks a club should be allowed.

3. Which of the following is an example of a good sentence to support your opinion? *The correct answer is C. This is a strong supporting sentence with a clear example as to a reason why the writer thinks phones should not be allowed at school.*

4. Sample Answer:

Baseball is my favorite sport. It has always been my favorite, because I think it is the most fun. First, it's good because you can watch it on TV or you can play it yourself, and it lasts all spring and summer. It's very fun and exciting to watch baseball games. At the game you can get popcorn or nachos and watch the game with your family or friends. You might even catch a fly ball. Second, baseball has been around in America since the late 1800s, so it's one of the oldest sports we have. Third, my favorite part of baseball is the team. When you win a game, you share it with the rest of your team. When you lose a game, you share that too. It's a good community game. And if you're watching baseball, it's fun to root for an entire team, even if you have a favorite player.

5. Sample Answer:

I have always wanted to travel to Florida. I have lived for my whole life in Maine, which is very cold for so much of the year. One winter, when it is 10 degrees, I would love to go down to Florida, because my mom told me that it sometimes is 80 degrees there in January. I'm not sure where in Florida I would go exactly, but I know there are a lot of choices. We could go see alligators in the Everglades, and they are my favorite animals. We would go to Disney World and EPCOT Center, or we could go to Cape Canaveral to see a rocket take off. We also could just sit on the beach and enjoy the hot sun and sand and ocean while my friends back home are wearing heavy coats! There are so many things to do in Florida, so I think it would be my favorite vacation.

THE STANDARD

W.4.5: *Planning and Revising*
With guidance and support from peers and adults, develop and strengthen writing as needed by planning, revising, and editing. (Editing for conventions should demonstrate command of Language standards 1-3 up to and including grade 4.)

What does it mean?

This writing standard focuses on a child's ability to improve upon his or her writing. The standard includes strategies for planning one's writing, as well as for revising the writing to make it clearer. The standard also focuses on editing for punctuation, spelling, grammar, and other writing conventions. As such, it is closely related to the Conventions of Standard English standards that are part of the Common Core Language skills. The fourth grade standards related to this are highlighted in the sidebar.

L.4.1 Demonstrate command of the conventions of standard English grammar and usage when writing or speaking.

- *L.4.1a* Use relative pronouns *(who, whose, whom, which, that)* and relative adverbs *(where, when, why)*.
- *L.4.1b* Form and use the progressive (e.g., *I was walking; I am walking; I will be walking)* verb tenses.
- *L.4.1c* Use modal auxiliaries (e.g., *can, may, must)* to convey various conditions.
- *L.4.1d* Order adjectives within sentences according to conventional patterns (e.g., *small red bag* rather than *a red small bag)*.
- *L.4.1e* Form and use prepositional phrases.
- *L.4.1f* Produce complete sentences, recognizing and correcting inappropriate fragments and run-ons.
- *L.4.1g* Correctly use frequently confused words (e.g., *to, too, two; there, their)*.

L.4.2 Demonstrate command of the conventions of standard English capitalization, punctuation, and spelling when writing.

- *L.4.2a* Use correct capitalization.
- *L.4.2b* Use commas and quotation marks to mark direct speech and quotations from a text.
- *L.4.2c* Spell grade-appropriate words correctly, consulting references as needed.
- *L.4.2d* Form and use possessives.

Try this together

In the previous lesson, you helped your child plan a piece of writing. This lesson will focus on the revising and editing stages of writing.

Explain that writing involves several steps. The revision process is when a writer looks back at the draft to improve upon it. Revising involves reading it to make sure that the main idea is clearly stated; that there are facts, definitions, and details supporting the main idea; that the organization makes sense; and that there is no extraneous information. Writers should also look for vague or overused words during the revision process to see if they can find other options.

Once all revisions have taken place, the draft is ready to be edited. It is during the editing process that a writer checks to make sure that the grammar, spelling, punctuation, and other language conventions are correct.

A checklist like the one on the following page can help your child revise and edit any piece of writing.

Before your child revises and edits the following paragraph, read through and familiarize yourself with the errors it contains. This will make it easier for you to be of assistance. Encourage your child to mark the paragraph while looking for ways to improve it. This can be done by circling or underlining certain parts of the text. Also suggest that the paragraph be read through several times to make sure that all errors are caught.

The Platypus

The Platypus about the stranggest animal you'll ever see. It has a bill and webbed feet like a duck, a tale like a beaver, and thick fur all over it's body. It also laid eggs, which is unusual for a mammel. A male Platypus can inject venom from barbs near its feet, and it's painful so do not try to pick one up one time at the zoo me and my Sister saw one, and it was very strange to see up close. That's all I have to say about the Platypus!

_____

_____

_____

_____

_____

_____

_____

_____

_____

Answers

Note that certain revision changes may vary from person to person.

The platypus is about the strangest animal you'll ever see. It has a bill and webbed feet like a duck, a tale like a beaver, and thick fur all over its body. It also lays eggs, which is unusual for a mammal. A male platypus can inject painful venom from barbs near its feet, so do not try to pick one up. One time at the zoo, my sister and I saw one, and it was very strange to view up close. With this combination of features, the platypus has got to be the strangest animal ever.

This exercise requires your child to make revisions and edits based on his or her understanding of clear and appropriate language usage. It also requires your child to understand the basic organization of a paragraph, with an introductory topic sentence that states your opinion, supporting details in the body, and a concluding sentence that sums up your main idea.

Extra practice

You and your child should each write a paragraph that expresses an opinion about something. Both paragraphs should purposely contain errors in spelling, punctuation, capitalization, and grammar. Then trade paragraphs and see if you can locate and correct the errors each other has added.

Revising and Editing Checklist	
Focus/Ideas	Does the report have a clear topic?
	Does the report stay on topic?
Organization	Are the ideas presented in a way that makes sense?
	Are ideas supported by facts, definitions, and details?
Conventions	Does the writer use correct grammar?
	Is the first word of each sentence capitalized? Are proper nouns (names of people and places) capitalized?
	Is there a period at the end of each sentence? Are commas, quotation marks, question marks, and other punctuation marks used correctly?
	Are all words spelled correctly?

Quiz

Have your child read the passage and then answer the questions that follow.

(1) Yesterday I baked chocolate chip cookies, which _____ my favorite. (2) First, I went to the store _____ I didn't have all the ingredients I needed. (3) After I got home, I mixed the ingredients together _____ a bowl: butter, sugar, eggs, vanilla, baking soda, chocolate chips, and flour. (4) After the dough was ready, I put the cookies in the oven and baked _____ for ten minutes. (5) Once they were baked, I took them out of the oven and put them over _____ on the counter to cool.

Questions

1. In sentence 1, which word is the best choice to fill in the blank?
   A. is   B. are   C. was   D. might

2. In sentence 2, which word is which word is the best choice to fill in the blank?
   A. but   B. if   C. why   D. because

3. In sentence 3, which word is the best choice to fill in the blank?
   A. in   B. on   C. with   D. before

4. In sentence 4, which word is the best choice to fill in the blank?
   A. it's   B. it   C. them   D. their

5. In sentence 5, which word is the best choice to fill in the blank?
   A. they're   B. their   C. there   D. then

Answers

1. In sentence 1, which word is the best choice to fill in the blank? *The correct answer is B. In the first sentence, your child should choose the correct verb form for the sentence. This is part of the "editing for conventions" element included in this standard.*

2. In sentence 2, which word is which word is the best choice to fill in the blank? *The correct answer is D. In the second sentence, your child should choose the correct conjunction for the sentence. This is part of the "editing for conventions" element included in this standard.*

3. In sentence 3, which word is the best choice to fill in the blank? *The correct answer is A. In the third sentence, your child should choose the correct preposition for the sentence to create a prepositional phrase. This is part of the "editing for conventions" element included in this standard.*

4. In sentence 4, which word is the best choice to fill in the blank? *The correct answer is C. In the fourth sentence, your child should choose the correct pronoun for the sentence.*

This is part of the "editing for conventions" element included in this standard.

5. In sentence 5, which word is the best choice to fill in the blank? *The correct answer is C. In the fifth sentence, your child must correctly choose from among similar and frequently confused words. This is part of the "editing for conventions" element included in this standard.*

OVERVIEW

For Grade 4, the Mathematics Common Core Standards focus heavily on two skill areas. The first skill area is multi-digit multiplication and division, using various models to illustrate the principles behind them. The second skill area is fractions, which covers adding, subtracting, and multiplying fractions.

Listed below are the Mathematics Common Core Standards for Grade 4 that we have identified as "power standards." We consider these standards to be critical for your child's success. Each lesson in this section focuses on a single standard (or set of related standards) so that you and your child may practice that specific skill to achieve mastery. The applicable standards are divided into three categories: Number & Operations in Base Ten; Operations & Algebraic Thinking; and Number & Operations—Fractions.

Number & Operations in Base Ten

Multi-Digit Multiplication with Area Models

> ***CCSS.Math.Content.4.NBT.B.5***: Multiply a whole number of up to four digits by a one-digit whole number, and multiply two two-digit numbers, using strategies based on place value and the properties of operations. Illustrate and explain the calculation by using equations, rectangular arrays, and/or area models.

Multi-Digit Multiplication with Properties of Operations and Place Value

> ***CCSS.Math.Content.4.NBT.B.5***: Multiply a whole number of up to four digits by a one-digit whole number, and multiply two two-digit numbers, using strategies based on place value and the properties of operations. Illustrate and explain the calculation by using equations, rectangular arrays, and/or area models.

> ***CCSS.Math.Content.4.NBT.A.1***: Recognize that in a multi-digit whole number, a digit in one

place represents ten times what it represents in the place to its right. For example, recognize that $700 \div 70 = 10$ by applying concepts of place value and division.

Division

CCSS.Math.Content.4.NBT.B.6: Find whole-number quotients and remainders with up to four-digit dividends and one-digit divisors, using strategies based on place value, the properties of operations, and/or the relationship between multiplication and division. Illustrate and explain the calculation by using equations, rectangular arrays, and/or area models.

Operations & Algebraic Thinking

Multi-Step Problems

CCSS.Math.Content.4.OA.A.3: Solve multistep word problems posed with whole numbers and having whole-number answers using the four operations, including problems in which remainders must be interpreted. Represent these problems using equations with a letter standing for the unknown quantity. Assess the reasonableness of answers using mental computation and estimation strategies including rounding.

Number & Operations—Fractions

Equivalent Fractions

CCSS.Math.Content.4.NF.A.1: Explain why a fraction a/b is equivalent to a fraction (n × a)/(n × b) by using visual fraction models, with attention to how the number and size of the parts differ even though the two fractions themselves are the same size. Use this principle to recognize and generate equivalent fractions.

Comparing Fractions

CCSS.Math.Content.4.NF.A.2: Compare two fractions with different numerators and different denominators, e.g., by creating common denominators or numerators, or by comparing to a benchmark fraction such as 1/2. Recognize that comparisons are valid only when the two fractions refer to the same whole. Record the results of comparisons with symbols >, =, or <, and justify the conclusions, e.g., by using a visual fraction model.

Adding and Subtracting Fractions

CCSS.Math.Content.4.NF.B.3: Understand a fraction a/b with a > 1 as a sum of fractions 1/b.

CCSS.Math.Content.4.NF.B.3a: Understand addition and subtraction of fractions as joining and separating parts referring to the same whole.

CCSS.Math.Content.4.NF.B.3b: Decompose a fraction into a sum of fractions with the same denominator in more than one way, recording each decomposition by an equation. Justify decompositions, e.g., by using a visual fraction model. Examples: 3/8 = 1/8 + 1/8 + 1/8 ; 3/8 = 1/8 + 2/8 ; 2 1/8 = 1 + 1 + 1/8 = 8/8 + 8/8 + 1/8.

CCSS.Math.Content.4.NF.B.3d: Solve word problems involving addition and subtraction of fractions referring to the same whole and having like denominators, e.g., by using visual fraction models and equations to represent the problem.

Adding and Subtracting Mixed Numbers

CCSS.Math.Content.4.NF.B.3a: Understand addition and subtraction of fractions as joining and separating parts referring to the same whole.

CCSS.Math.Content.4.NF.B.3c: Add and subtract mixed numbers with like denominators, e.g., by replacing each mixed number with an equivalent fraction, and/or by using properties of operations and the relationship between addition and subtraction.

CCSS.Math.Content.4.NF.B.3d: Solve word problems involving addition and subtraction of fractions referring to the same whole and having like denominators, e.g., by using visual fraction models and equations to represent the problem.

Multiplying Unit Fractions and Whole Numbers

CCSS.Math.Content.4.NF.B.4: Apply and extend previous understandings of multiplication to multiply a fraction by a whole number.

CCSS.Math.Content.4.NF.B.4a: Understand a fraction a/b as a multiple of $1/b$. For example, use a visual fraction model to represent 5/4 as the product $5 \times (1/4)$, recording the conclusion by the equation $5/4 = 5 \times (1/4)$.

Multiplying Fractions and Whole Numbers

CCSS.Math.Content.4.NF.B.4b: Understand a multiple of a/b as a multiple of $1/b$, and use this understanding to multiply a fraction by a whole number. For example, use a visual fraction model to express $3 \times (2/5)$ as $6 \times (1/5)$, recognizing this product as 6/5. (In general, $n \times (a/b) = (n \times a)/b$.)

CCSS.Math.Content.4.NF.B.4c: Solve word problems involving multiplication of a fraction by a whole number, e.g., by using visual fraction models and equations to represent the problem. For example, if each person at a party will eat 3/8 of a pound of roast beef, and there will be 5 people at the party, how many pounds of roast beef will be needed? Between what two whole numbers does your answer lie?

THE STANDARD

4.NBT.B.5: Multiply a whole number of up to four digits by a one-digit whole number, and multiply two two-digit numbers, using strategies based on place value and the properties of operations. Illustrate and explain the calculation by using equations, rectangular arrays, and/or area models.

What does it mean?

Under this standard, students take their understanding of multiplication with single digits and apply it to multiplying larger numbers. The main focus is on strategies using a visual model such as arrays or area models to understand the mechanics of the process.

Try this together

At this stage, it is assumed that children have memorized all the two digit multiplication combinations (the common "multiplication tables"). With this background knowledge, they can begin to approach more complicated multiplication problems such as 34×45 or 18×60. The strategies that students can use are varied and they are not expected to use the standard multiplication algorithm until grade 5.

The different strategies all center around the idea of "breaking up" a number using an understanding of place value. Not only does this help students get a feel for the process itself, it also helps them develop a deeper understanding of the distributive property, which is studied more closely in later grades.

In previous grades, students would use arrays to represent multiplication. An array with 3 rows and 9 columns can be used to represent 3×9=27.

```
* * * * * * * * *
* * * * * * * * *
* * * * * * * * *
```

Students should also understand that a rectangle that is 3 units wide and 9 units long has an area of 27 square units. This can be shown by breaking it up into squares.

An area model for multiplication with more digits is similar. To multiply 34×45, first think of a rectangle that is 34 units long and 45 units wide. It would not make sense to draw all of these unit squares! Break up the tens and ones in each number: 34=30+4 and 45=40+5, then multiply to find the area of each smaller rectangle. So an area model for this problem would be:

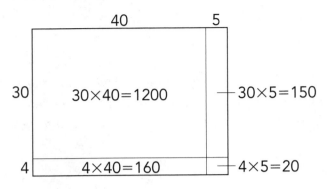

The area of this rectangle is 34 × 45 is the same as the area of all of the rectangles inside it added together. So 34×45=1,200+160+150+20=1,530.

Let's look at each of the smaller rectangles more closely. The bottom right rectangle is 5 units long and 4 units tall, so its area is 20 square units because 5×4=20. The top right rectangle is 5 units by 30 units, or 5 units multiplied by 3 tens. The product is 15 tens or 150. The bottom left rectangle is 4 units by 4 tens, or 16 tens, which equals 160. Finally, when tens are multiplied together, the product is in hundreds. The top left rectangle is 3 tens × 4 tens=12 hundreds or 1,200.

As you practice problems with your child, focus on breaking the numbers up using place value. Help your child use the word "product" to describe the result of multiplication (for example, the product of 6 and 7 is 42) and the word "equation" to describe a mathematical sentence with an equal sign (for example, 6×7 is not an equation, but 6×7=42 and 6×7=40+2 are both equations).

 Quiz

1. Write an equation to represent the area model.

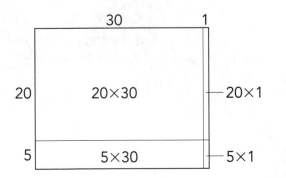

2. Write an equation to represent the area model.

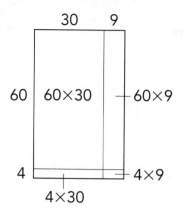

3. Find the product of 48 and 13. Draw an area model to show your work.

4. Find the product of 27 and 95. Draw an area model to show your work.

5. Using the area model, which equation is true?

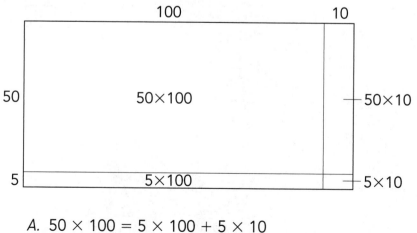

A. $50 \times 100 = 5 \times 100 + 5 \times 10$

B. $55 \times 110 = 50 \times 100 + 50 \times 10$

C. $55 \times 110 = 50 \times 100 + 50 \times 10 + 5 \times 100 + 5 \times 10$

D. $50 \times 100 = 50 \times 100 + 50 \times 10 + 5 \times 10$

✓ Answers

1. Write an equation to represent the area model.

   The correct answer is 25×31=775.

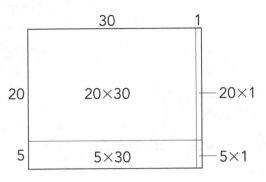

The width of the rectangle is 20+5=25 while the length is 30+1=31. To find the total area, find the area of each rectangle: 20×30=600, 5×30=150, 20×1=20, 5×1=5, and then add: 600+150+20+5=755.

Questions 1 and 2 help your child develop a deeper understanding of area models by seeing models that are already created for them. Help them to understand the relationship between the numbers being multiplied in the large rectangle (like 31 and 25), and each small rectangle.

2. Write an equation to represent the area model.
   The correct answer is 64×39=2,496.

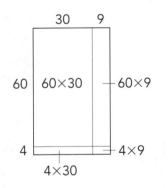

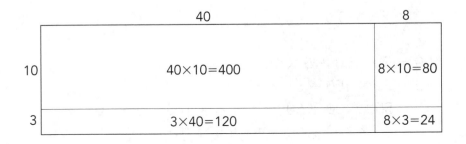

The width of the rectangle is 60+4=64 while the length is 30+9=39. Therefore the total area find the area of each rectangle: 60×30=1,800, 60×9=540, 4×30=120, 4×9=36, and then add: 1,800+540+120+36=2,496.

3. Find the product of 48 and 13. Draw an area model to show your work.
   The correct answer is 624.
   400+120+80+24=624.

   This question gives your child the opportunity to practice breaking up numbers to find products by drawing area models. Children may be asked to create models like this on tests.

4. Find the product of 27 and 95. Draw an area model to show your work.
   The correct answer is 2,565.

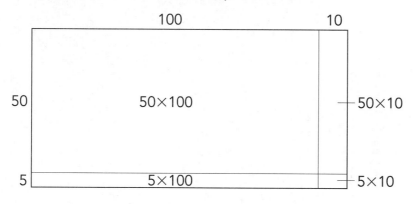

1,800+630+100+35=2,565.

This question gives your child the opportunity to practice breaking up numbers to find products by drawing area models. Children may be asked to create models like this on tests.

5. Using the area model, which equation is true?

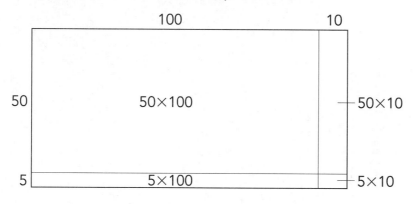

A. 50×100=5×100+5×10
B. 55×110=50×100+50×10
C. 55×110=50×100+50×10 + 5×100 + 5×10
D. 50×100=50×100+50×10+5×10

The correct answer is C.

The overall area is the total area of each of the smaller rectangles. Remember that the

Order of Operations says that multiplication comes before addition, so no parentheses are needed.

It is important that your child understand that the area model uses areas from all portions of the rectangle. Questions like #5 make sure that they can see when this is done correctly using mathematical symbols and language.

THE STANDARD

4.NBT.B.5: Multiply a whole number of up to four digits by a one-digit whole number, and multiply two two-digit numbers, using strategies based on place value and the properties of operations. Illustrate and explain the calculation by using equations, rectangular arrays, and/or area models.

4.NBT.A.1: Recognize that in a multi-digit whole number, a digit in one place represents ten times what it represents in the place to its right. For example, recognize that $700 \div 70 = 10$ by applying concepts of place value and division.

What does it mean?

This pair of standards addresses ideas that come up when working with area models in multiplication. These models require that a child be able to write numbers and multiplication problems in different forms. The techniques they need to use to accomplish this are based on place value and a strong understanding of its deeper meaning in terms of the size of a number.

Try this together

Place value is an important concept, and without it children will have difficulty in understanding advanced multiplication and division problems. The key is for your child to know the difference between the value of 2 in a number like 152 and in a number like 1,230. In the first number, the 2 is in the ones place, so it represents 2 ones whereas in the second number, it is in the hundreds place and so it represents 2 hundreds.

This is useful in working with multiplication because it implies that multiplying by 10 results in shifting each digit in a number one place to the left. So, $5 \times 10 = 50$. Similarly, multiplying by 100 moves a number two places to the left, so $8 \times 100 = 800$. Students can take this further when working with products like $6 \times 2,000$ by thinking of it as $6 \times 2 \times 1,000 = 12 \times 1,000 = 12,000$ because multiplying by 1,000 results in moving the number 3 places to the left.

When working with more complex multiplication problems, your child can use his or her understanding with working with these numbers to make a strategy for how to break up any pair of numbers. For example, in the multiplication problem 249×8, the 249 can be viewed as $200 + 40 + 9$ and the problem rewritten as $(200 + 40 + 9) \times 8$. Now, by the distributive property, the final answer is 200 × 8 + 40 × 8 + 9 × 8 = 1,600 + 320 + 72 = 1,992.

This is a powerful strategy for multiplying 2 to 4 digit numbers by a single digit number. Practice it with your child to help her develop mental math skills general number sense. This will also help her when she learns the standard algorithm (regular steps) for multiplying in fifth grade.

Quiz

1. Which of these expressions has the same value as 104 × 10?
   A. (100 + 4) × 10   B. (100 × 4) × 10
   C. (100 + 4) × (5 × 5)   D. (100 × 4) + 10

2. Which of these expressions has the same value as 6,201 × 6?
   A. 6,000 × 6 + 200 × 6
   B. 6,000 × 6 + 200 × 6 + 1 × 6
   C. 6,000 × 6 + 200 × 6 × 1 × 6
   D. 6,000 × 6 × 200 × 6 × 1 × 6

3. Which of these expressions has the same value as 78 × 85?
   A. (70 + 8) × (80 × 5)
   B. (70 × 8) × (80 × 5)
   C. (70 + 8) × (80 + 5)
   D. (70 × 8) × (80 + 5)

4. Find the product of 2,500 and 8 by breaking the numbers into smaller parts. Show your work.

5. Find the product of 964 and 4 by breaking the numbers into smaller parts. Show your work.

Answers

1. Which of these expressions has the same value as 104 × 10?
   A. (100 + 4) × 10   B. (100 × 4) × 10
   C. (100 + 4) × (5 × 5)   D. (100 × 4) + 10

The correct answer is A.

Here, 104 = 100 + 4 and so 104 × 10 = (100 + 4) × 10.

Questions 1, 2, and 3 test your child's ability to break up factors in a multiplication problem, which is the first step toward multiplying large numbers. If your child struggles with these skills, you may want to use place value charts to label the thousands, hundreds, tens, and ones digits, and return to the area models from lesson 1.

2. Which of these expressions has the same value as 6,201 × 6?
   A. 6,000 × 6 + 200 × 6
   B. 6,000 × 6 + 200 × 6 + 1 × 6
   C. 6,000 × 6 + 200 × 6 + 10 × 6
   D. 6,000 × 6 × 200 × 6 × 10 × 6

The correct answer is B.

It is important to notice that the 1 is in the ones place. Therefore, the correct answer cannot be C or D. which treat it as though it is in the tens place. Answer A is missing this part of the number completely.

3. Which of these expressions has the same value as 78 × 85?
   A. (70 + 8) × (80 × 5)   B. (70 × 8) × (80 × 5)
   C. (70 + 8) × (80 + 5)   D. (70 × 8) × (80 + 5)

The correct answer is C.

In this problem, each number is broken up using place value. 78 = 70 + 8 and 85 = 80 + 5. Breaking up the numbers by place value does not change their product.

4. Find the product of 2,500 and 8.

The correct answer is 20,000.

The number 2,500 can be broken up into 2000 + 500 and then multiplied by 8 to get 2,500 × 8 = (2000+500) × 8 = 2,000 × 8 + 500 × 8 = 16,000 + 4,000 = 20,000.

Questions 4 and 5 give your child an opportunity to try all of the steps of the problem independently. Ultimately this will lead to an easier time with applying the standard algorithm to more complex problems.

5. Find the product of 964 and 4.

The correct answer is 3,856.

Because 964 = 900 + 60 + 4, the product can be found using 964 × 4 = (900 + 60 +4) × 4 = 900 × 4 + 60 × 4 + 4 × 4 = 3,600 + 240 + 16 = 3,856.

THE STANDARD

4.NBT.B.6: Find whole-number quotients and remainders with up to four-digit dividends and one-digit divisors, using strategies based on place value, the properties of operations, and/or the relationship between multiplication and division. Illustrate and explain the calculation by using equations, rectangular arrays, and/or area models.

What does it mean?

Students at this level are expected to be able to divide four digit numbers by a single digit number accurately. In order to get a conceptual understanding of the process, they use models such as the area and array models and study the connection between division and multiplication.

Try this together

Many of the models and skills your child learned when working with multiplication can be carried over to division. For instance, when applying place value strategies to multiplication, your child may have thought of 430×2 as $2 \times 400 + 30 \times 2$. Alternatively, your child might have found 43×2 and then multiplied by 10.

From memorizing the multiplication tables, your child should already be comfortable with a division question such as $24 \div 6$. Using place value, this can be connected to division problems such as $240 \div 6$. Think of 240 as 24 tens, and then divide the tens into 6 equal groups. There are 4 tens in each group, so the quotient (answer in the division problem) is 40.

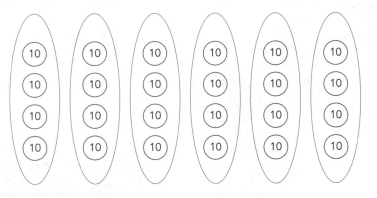

With an area model, the dividend (the number being divided) is thought of as the area of a rectangle, and the divisor (number doing the dividing) is a side length. The division problem can then be thought of as finding an unknown side length. The division problem 1351 ÷ 7 could be represented with the following picture.

Area: 1351

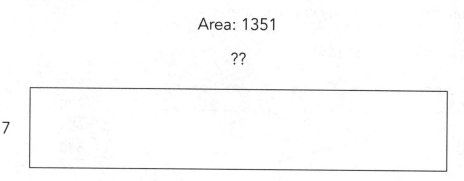

Taken further, the unknown side length can be broken up into a certain number of hundreds, tens, and ones.

Area: 1351

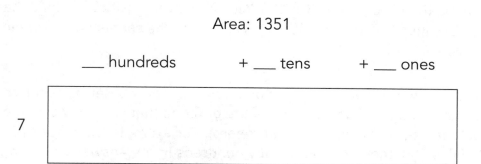

Now your child can think of the division in pieces. Start with the hundreds. Multiplying 7 by 1 hundred gives 700, which is less than 1,351 so could fit. Multiplying 7 by 2 hundreds gives 1,400, which is bigger than the area of 1,351. So there can only be 1 hundred. Label the area of the smaller rectangle inside:

Area: 1351

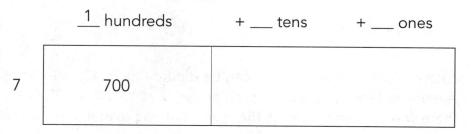

The area that is left is 1,351 − 700 = 651. You can fit in 9 tens because 90 × 7 = 630, which is less than 651. In the next step, write "9 tens" at the top, and create a new rectangle inside with the area of 630.

This leaves an area of 651 − 630 = 21, which students should recognize as 3 × 7. A complete area model is shown below including one method to keep track of the subtraction. Your child can subtract each area piece as they go using a method that is very similar to the classic long division method they will use later.

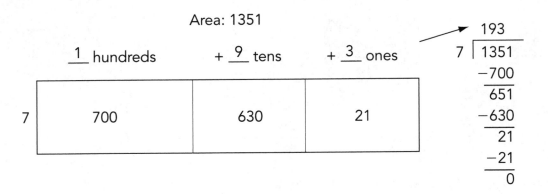

The final answer is then 100 + 90 + 3 = 193. You should verify with your child that the area would be 1,351 because 7 × 193 = 1,351. This reaffirms the connection between multiplication and division.

Eventually, students working with this type of division will encounter remainders. Conceptually these can be thought of as a portion of the dividend that can't be accounted for with the area model (at least not using whole numbers). For example, consider 412 ÷ 5. First, because 5 × 100 is 500, there will not be any hundreds in the answer. So our answer will be made up of tens and ones.

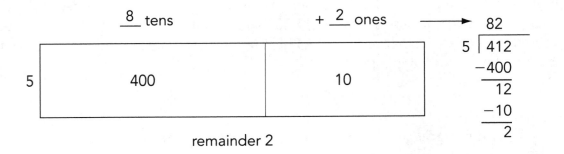

As a number sentence, this shows how 412 can be thought of as 410 plus 2 more, or 5 × 82 + 2. This is similar to how the previous problem showed that 7 × 193 = 1,351. In that case however, there was no remainder, so there was nothing to add to the left hand side.

With these division problems, it is important to help your child develop a firm conceptual grasp through using the different models. In fourth grade, they should not worry about using a formal long division process and can focus on developing their own overall approach and understanding.

? Quiz

1. If the area of the rectangle below is 4800, then what is the length of the rectangle?

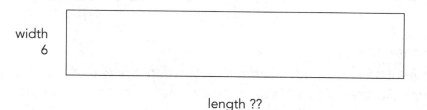

width
6

length ??

2. If 3,323 = 830 × 4 + 3, then what is the remainder for the division problem 3,323 ÷ 4?
   A. 3323　　　　B. 830　　　　C. 4　　　　D. 3

3. If 56 × 9 = 504, then what is 504 ÷ 9?
   A. 9　　　　B. 56　　　　C. 495　　　　D. 504

4. Randall has 1,025 pieces of paper to use in each of 5 months. If he uses the same number each month, then how many will he use? Show your work using an area model.

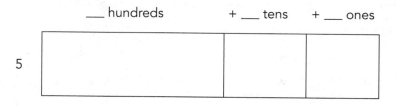

___ hundreds　　+ ___ tens　　+ ___ ones

5

5. There are 296 days until Katy leaves for a trip. If there are 7 days a week, then how many weeks are there until Katy leaves for her trip? Show your work using an area model.

✓ Answers

1. If the area of the rectangle below is 4800, then what is the correct length of the rectangle?

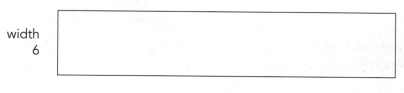

width
6

length ??

The correct answer is 800.

Your child should have 6 × 8 = 48 memorized and therefore quickly see that 4800 ÷ 6 is 48 hundreds divided by 6. This would result in 8 hundreds.

This question checks your child's concept of division as a missing-length problem where the number being divided is the area.

2. If 3323 = 830 × 4 + 3, then what is the remainder for the division problem 3323 ÷ 4?

   A. 3323   B. 830   C. 4   D. 3

   The correct answer is D.

   The answer here should be done without calculation. Instead, through practice with area models, your child should be able to recognize that this is the way that a number can be written when the quotient and remainder for a problem like this is known.

   Questions 2 and 3 ask your child to represent the connection between multiplication and division using a number sentence. As you and your child work on any division problem, it is useful to write these number sentences for any answer that you get and make sure that the connection is understood.

3. If 56 × 9 = 504, then what is 504 ÷ 9?

   A. 9   B. 56   C. 495   D. 504

   The correct answer is B.

   Through the connection between multiplication and division, 56 × 9 = 504 implies that 504 ÷ 9 = 56 and 504 ÷ 56 = 9.

4. Randall has 1,025 pieces of paper to use in each of 5 months. If he uses the same number each month, then how many will he use? Show your work using an area model.

   The correct answer is 205 pieces.

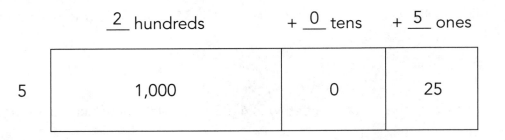

   In the area model, there are 2 hundreds because 200 × 5 = 1,000, which leaves 25 remaining. If you multiplied 5 × 1 ten, the result would be 50, which is larger than 25, so there are no tens. To make 25, multiply 5 × 5 ones.

   Questions 4 and 5 ask your child to perform all of the steps of a division problem himself, showing and explaining his work. Focus on the use of place value and dividing using facts from the multiplication table and then multiplying by ones, tens, hundreds, and thousands.

5. There are 296 days until Katy leaves for a trip. If there are 7 days a week, then how many weeks are there until Katy leaves for her trip?

The correct answer is 42 weeks and 2 days.

	_0_ hundreds	+ _4_ tens	+ _2_ ones	
7	0	40×7=280	2×7=14	+2 more

This can be thought of as dividing the 296 days into equal groups of 7. There are 294 ÷ 7 = 42 groups of seven days (weeks) plus 2 extra days. Using an area model, your child should notice that there must be 4 tens in the answer because 40 × 7 = 280. This leaves 16, which is equal to 2 × 7 = 14, plus 2 ones left over.

THE STANDARD

4.OA.A.3: Solve multistep word problems posed with whole numbers and having whole-number answers using the four operations, including problems in which remainders must be interpreted. Represent these problems using equations with a letter standing for the unknown quantity. Assess the reasonableness of answers using mental computation and estimation strategies including rounding.

What does it mean?

Being able to apply the basic operations of mathematics to solve real world problems is the focus of this standard. In addition to being able to find a correct answer, students are expected to be able to interpret the abstract concept of a remainder in division problems and use estimation to determine if an answer makes sense in the real life situation.

Try this together

To be successful with solving multi-step word problems, your child must learn to approach them systematically and pay attention to clues that show which operation is needed. Problems for this standard may use addition, subtraction, multiplication, division, or a combination of these. Most importantly, your child needs to be able to assess how reasonable his or her answer is instead of simply applying the math and not double checking.

There are plenty of real life situations which you can use to help your child understand the different approaches to these types of problems. For instance, suppose you and your family went on a 5-day road trip. On the first day, you drove 120 miles. On the second day, you drove 370 miles. Finally, for each of the next three days, you drove 295 miles. The question you could ask your child is "How many miles did we drive in total?"

The key idea here is that the total is needed. Totals are found using multiplication and/or addition. Regardless of the type of operation used, the approach should always be carefully thought out. Here, a table could be made showing each day.

day 1	day 2	day 3	day 4	day 5
120	370	295	295	295

Now, it is simple to see that the total is 120 + 370 + 295 + 295 + 295 = 1375 miles. Another approach would be to total the first two days 120+370 = 490 and then use multiplication to find the total in the last three days 295 × 3 = 885. The overall total would be 885 + 490 = 1375.

Whichever approach is used to a word problem like this, you should always discuss the idea of reasonableness. One way to check reasonableness is to round the numbers and do a rough calculation. Day 1's travel could be thought of as about 100 miles while day 2's is about 400 miles. This brings the total to 500 miles. Now the next 3 days were about 300 miles each, and 3 × 300 = 900. So the total should be around 500 + 900 = 1,400 miles. Any number far off from this should indicate to your child that the problem should be revisited.

In division problems, there are many ways to approach the remainder and again, all of them have real life examples. To see this, we will use a problem that is only one step but focus on the remainder and its meaning. Suppose that your child wants to bring 42 cupcakes to class, and boxes hold 12 cupcakes each. How many boxes will be needed? Your child should be able to determine that division is needed here and that 42 ÷ 12 = 3 remainder 6. This means that if 3 boxes are used they will be completely filled but there will still be 6 cupcakes that are left over. Therefore, 4 boxes would be needed to carry all of the cupcakes.

To help your child to be successful on these problems, start by having him underline clues which tell which operation to use (+, −, ×, or ÷) and underline the numbers that go with them. Then, have him write equations for each one. The more work he can show, the more you can talk together about the decisions he's making for solving the problems.

Quiz

1. Sachen is allowed to watch 30 minutes of TV every school day and 60 minutes every weekend day. If a month has 31 total days and 20 of them are school days, then how many minutes of TV is he allowed to watch that month?

2. Ms. Barenboim's class is selling candy bars for a fundraiser and needs to sell 400 for a field trip. On the first day, students sold 3 boxes and on the second day, they sold 5 more boxes. If each box has 10 candy bars, then how many candy bars do they still need to sell?

3. A farmer has 52 chickens. On Saturday, he gave 2 chickens to one friend and on Sunday he gave 10 chickens to a different friend. If he has to buy 2 pounds of chicken feed

for each of the remaining chickens, then how much chicken feed does he need to buy?

4. Carrie's book collection is made up of 35 books and each shelf on her bookshelf will hold 8 books. If her aunt gives her 4 new books, how many shelves will Carrie need for her whole collection?

5. Last year, Gary's grandfather gave him $25 for his birthday. Since then, Gary has saved his $3 a week allowance for 6 weeks. He wants to buy some cards that cost $4 each. If he buys as many cards as he can afford, how many cards can he buy? How much money will he have left?

✓ **Answers**

1. Sachen is allowed to watch 30 minutes of TV every school day and 60 minutes every weekend day. If a month has 31 total days and 20 of them are school days, then how many minutes of TV is he allowed to watch that month?
The correct answer is 1,260 minutes.
The 20 school days will result in $20 \times 30 = 600$ minutes of TV allowed, but the trick is to figure out the number of other days. Since the month is 31 days long, there are $31 - 20 = 11$ days without school. On these days, Sachen is allowed to watch $11 \times 60 = 660$ minutes of TV for a total of $600 + 660 = 1,260$ minutes.
This question requires your child to see that some information is not given directly. Specifically, they should see that they need to find the number of days that there is not school in the month based on the total number of days given for that month. Problems like this are good practice for paying attention to all aspects of the situation.

2. Ms. Barenboim's class is selling candy bars for a fundraiser and needs to sell 400 for a field trip. On the first day, students sold 3 boxes and on the second day, they sold 5 more boxes. If each box has 10 candy bars, then how many candy bars do they still need to sell?
The correct answer is 320.
The total number of candy bars sold so far is $3 \times 10 + 5 \times 10 = 30 + 50 = 80$. This means that $400 - 80 = 320$ still must be sold.
This question involves multiplication combined with subtraction but in different orders. This helps your child see that the order matters and that it depends on the context.

3. A farmer has 52 chickens. On Saturday, he gave 2 chickens to one friend and on Sunday he gave 10 chickens to a different friend. If he has to buy 2 pounds of chicken feed for each of the remaining chickens, then how much chicken feed does he need to buy?
The correct answer is 80 pounds.

After giving chickens to his friends, the farmer is left with $52 - 2 - 10 = 40$ chickens. Since he needs 2 pounds of chicken feed for each chicken, he will need $40 \times 2 = 80$ pounds of feed.

This question involves multiplication combined with subtraction but in different orders. This helps your child see that the order matters and that it depends on the context.

4. Carrie's book collection is made up of 35 books and each shelf on her bookshelf will hold 8 books. If her aunt gives her 4 new books, how many shelves will Carrie need for her whole collection?
The correct answer is 5 shelves.

After the gift from her aunt, Carrie has 39 books. Because each book holds 8 books and $39 \div 8 = 4$ remainder 7, she will need 5 shelves. Note that only 4 of the shelves will be completely filled while the last one will have only 7 books.

Questions 4 and 5 require careful thought about what the quotient and remainder mean in a problem. In question 4, the answer is 4 shelves with 7 books left over, but because the books need to go somewhere, 5 shelves are needed. A picture of the actual shelf and the books is a great way to help with the understanding of this idea.

5. Last year, Gary's grandfather gave him $25 for his birthday. Since then, Gary has saved his $3 a week allowance for 6 weeks. He wants to buy some cards that cost $4 each. If he buys as many cards as he can afford, how many cards can he buy? How much money will he have left?
The correct answer is 9 cards and $1 left.

Gary has saved a total of $3 \times 6 = \$18$ from his allowance. Adding this to his birthday gift, he has $18 + 25 = \$37$ total saved. Use division to find the number of cards he can buy: $37 \div 4 = 9$ R 1, so he can buy 9 cards and he will have $1 left.

Questions 4 and 5 require careful thought about what the quotient and remainder mean in a problem. In question 5, the number of cards he can buy is the quotient and the money left is the remainder.

THE STANDARD

4.NF.A.1: Explain why a fraction $\frac{a}{b}$ is equivalent to a fraction $\frac{(n \times a)}{(n \times b)}$ by using visual fraction models, with attention to how the number and size of the parts differ even though the two fractions themselves are the same size. Use this principle to recognize and generate equivalent fractions.

What does it mean?

In third grade, children generated equivalent fractions using fraction models. In fourth grade, they are expanding this understanding by connecting multiplication to the models. Work under this standard is limited to fractions with the denominators 2, 3, 4, 5, 6, 8, 10, and 12.

Try this together

In a fraction $\frac{a}{b}$, b is the denominator and it represents the total number of parts in the whole. The numerator, a, represents the number of parts that are selected. For example, if 10 cookies are baked and 5 are eaten, you can write that $\frac{5}{10}$ or $\frac{1}{2}$ of the cookies were eaten. These bar models show that $\frac{5}{10}$ and $\frac{1}{2}$ are equivalent fractions because the same part of the whole is shaded in both.

Notice that if you start with the bar model of $\frac{1}{2}$ and then divide each section into 5 parts, there are 5 times as many parts. This is like multiplying the denominator by 5. To keep showing the same fraction, 5 times as many parts need to be shaded, which is like multiplying the numerator by 5.

You can write this as an equation: $\frac{1 \times 5}{2 \times 5} = \frac{5}{10}$.

Mathematically, you can explain this by remembering that when you multiply any number by

1, the result is the same number: $\frac{1}{2} \times 1 = \frac{1}{2}$. And any fraction with the same numerator and denominator is equal to 1, so $\frac{5}{5} = 1$. So multiplying a fraction by $\frac{5}{5}$ is the same as multiplying by 1, and the result has the same value.

Other fractions equivalent to $\frac{1}{2}$ can also be found by multiplying by fractions that have the same numerator and denominator: $\frac{3}{6} = \frac{1 \times 3}{2 \times 3}$ and $\frac{4}{8} = \frac{1 \times 4}{2 \times 4}$.

Equivalent fractions can also be shown on a number line. For instance, $\frac{1}{3}$ can be shown on the number line by dividing the space between 0 and 1 into 3 equal parts and then moving over 1 part to the right of 0. Because $\frac{1 \times 2}{3 \times 2} = \frac{2}{6}$, $\frac{1}{3}$ and $\frac{2}{6}$ are equivalent fractions. This can be seen on the number line by dividing each of the spaces on the number line into two equal parts to get a total of 6 pieces between 0 and 1 and then moving over 2 spaces to the right of 0.

Your child should also be able to perform this operation in reverse. Because dividing any amount by 1 gives the same value, dividing the numerator and denominator of a fraction by the same number creates an equivalent fraction. In this case, your child should look for a common factor, or number that both the numerator and denominator are divisible by.

$$\frac{5 \div 5}{10 \div 5} = \frac{1}{2} \qquad \frac{2 \div 2}{6 \div 2} = \frac{1}{3}$$

Under this standard, your child should be able to give examples of equivalent fractions and use either of the models above to show that two fractions are equivalent. As you work with him or her, be sure to consistently use both models and the idea of multiplying the numerator and the denominator by the same value.

❓ Quiz

1. Which of the following fractions is equivalent to the fraction below?

A. $\frac{2}{3}$ B. $\frac{4}{8}$ C. $\frac{2}{4}$ D. $\frac{4}{12}$

2. What number in place of the question mark makes the number sentence below true?

$$\frac{1\times?}{5\times2}=\frac{2}{10}$$

3. Which of the following fractions is equivalent to $\frac{12}{10}$?

A. $\frac{10}{8}$
   B. $\frac{6}{5}$
   C. $\frac{2}{10}$
   D. $\frac{7}{5}$

4. Find three fractions that are equivalent to $\frac{1}{2}$. Show your work with bar models and equations.

5. Find two fractions that are equivalent to $\frac{5}{4}$. Show your work with number lines and equations.

✓ Answers

1. Which of the following fractions is equivalent to the fraction represented below?

A. $\frac{2}{3}$
   B. $\frac{4}{8}$
   C. $\frac{2}{4}$
   D. $\frac{4}{12}$

The correct answer is D.

The fraction shown is $\frac{2}{6}$. Looking at the answer choices, $\frac{4}{12}$ can be generated by multiplying the numerator and the denominator by the same number, 2, or by dividing each part of the model into 2 equal parts. You can also think of this as multiplying $\frac{4}{12}\times\frac{2}{2}$.

Another equivalent fraction is $\frac{1}{3}$, which is generated by dividing the numerator and de-

nominator by 2. However, this is not an available answer.

This question can help your child make a bridge between third grade strategies of finding equivalent fractions using only models and using those models to understand the role of multiplying or dividing both the numerator and denominator by the same number.

2. What number in place of the question mark makes the number sentence below true?

$$\frac{1\times?}{5\times2}=\frac{2}{10}$$

The correct answer is 2.

To generate an equivalent fraction, the numerator and the denominator must be multiplied by the same number.

It is important that your child understand that to generate an equivalent fraction, the numerator and the denominator must be multiplied by the same value. This question gets them thinking about this idea. One area of discussion would be to use a number other than 2 in place of the question mark and then using a visual model to show that the resulting fraction is not equivalent.

3. Which of the following fractions is equivalent to $\frac{12}{10}$?

   A. $\frac{10}{8}$ 　　　　 B. $\frac{6}{5}$ 　　　　 C. $\frac{2}{10}$ 　　　　 D. $\frac{7}{5}$

The correct answer is B.

If the numerator and denominator of $\frac{12}{10}$ are both divided by 2, the result is $\frac{6}{5}$. This problem can also be solved by starting with the answer choices: if the numerator and the denominator of $\frac{6}{5}$ are both multiplied by 2, then the equivalent fraction $\frac{12}{10}$ is generated.

This question gives your child the chance to solve a basic equivalence problem using a strategy of his or her choice. Your child might solve it using a bar model or number line, by finding a common factor for 12 and 10 and dividing by it, or by multiplying each answer choice by fractions equivalent to 1 to see if one of them is equivalent.

Notice also that the fraction $\frac{12}{10}$ is greater than 1 because the numerator is greater than the denominator. Your child should be equally comfortable with fractions less than and greater than 1.

4. Find three fractions that are equivalent to $\frac{1}{2}$. Show your work with bar models and equations.

Sample correct answers are:

$$\frac{1\times2}{2\times2}=\frac{2}{4}$$

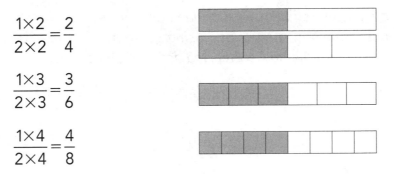

$$\frac{1\times3}{2\times3}=\frac{3}{6}$$

$$\frac{1\times4}{2\times4}=\frac{4}{8}$$

To find equivalent fractions, multiply the numerator and denominator by the same number, or divide each of the parts of the bar into the same number of parts.

Questions 4 and 5 are testing your child's ability to use the common visual models. While discussing these, it may be useful to show the other model (the number line for 4, and the bar model for 5) to reiterate that either model can be used to show the same thing. Question 5 is a bit more difficult because the fraction is greater than 1, and because equivalent fractions can be found using division as well as multiplication.

5. Find two fractions that are equivalent to $\frac{5}{4}$. Show your work with number lines and equations.

$$\frac{6\div2}{4\div2}=\frac{3}{2}$$

$$\frac{6\times2}{4\times2}=\frac{12}{8}$$

The fraction $\frac{6}{4}$ has a numerator that is larger than its denominator, so it is greater than 1. To show it on a number line, each whole (from 0 to 1 and then from 1 to 2) should be divided into 4 equal parts. Then, count 6 spaces to the right of the 0.

To find an equivalent fraction, multiply or divide the denominator by the same number. Both 6 and 4 are divisible by 2, so dividing by 2 is a good choice. To show this on the number line, either divide each space into the same number of parts, or combine spaces with the same amount of space in each part.

THE STANDARD

4.NF.A.2: Compare two fractions with different numerators and different denominators, e.g., by creating common denominators or numerators, or by comparing to a benchmark fraction such as $\frac{1}{2}$. Recognize that comparisons are valid only when the two fractions refer to the same whole. Record the results of comparisons with symbols >, =, or <, and justify the conclusions, e.g., by using a visual fraction model.

What does it mean?

In third grade, children learned how to compare fractions (determine which is greater, or if they are equal) by drawing models of each fraction and then visually comparing them by size, or by noticing rules for fractions with common numerators or denominators. In fourth grade, they are expected to compare fractions with different numerators and denominators using estimations based on how close the numerator and denominator are to each other, or by creating common numerators or denominators. At this level, denominators of fractions are limited to 2, 3, 4, 5, 6, 8, 10, 12, and 100.

Try this together

In third grade, students learned to compare fractions two ways: using models, and using common numerators or common denominators. For example, in this bar model, it can be seen that $\frac{4}{8}$ is less than $\frac{2}{3}$ because $\frac{4}{8}$ represents a smaller part of the whole. On the number line, $\frac{4}{8}$ is farther to the left than $\frac{2}{3}$, so it is less. This comparison is written $\frac{4}{8} < \frac{2}{3}$. Students can think of the < and > symbols as hungry alligators whose open mouths face the larger number.

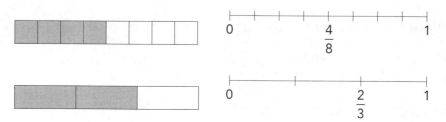

In fourth grade, students should also be able to look at these two fractions and compare them in two new ways: using benchmark fractions and converting the fractions to have like numerators or denominators.

To use benchmark fractions, students make an estimate of whether each fraction is close to 0, $\frac{1}{2}$ or 1, following these rules:

- If the denominator is much greater than the numerator, the fraction is close to 0. Examples: $\frac{1}{4}$, $\frac{2}{10}$, $\frac{3}{12}$

- If the denominator is about or exactly two times the numerator, the fraction is close to $\frac{1}{2}$. Examples: $\frac{2}{5}$, $\frac{5}{8}$, $\frac{6}{12}$

- If the denominator is only a little bit greater than the numerator, the fraction is close to 1. Examples: $\frac{3}{4}$, $\frac{7}{8}$, $\frac{10}{12}$

Using our example above, in the fraction $\frac{4}{8}$, the denominator is exactly two times the numerator ($4 \times 2 = 8$) so this is a fraction equal to $\frac{1}{2}$. The fraction $\frac{2}{3}$ has a denominator that is only a little bit greater than the numerator, so the fraction is closer to 1. A fraction close to $\frac{1}{2}$ is less than a fraction close to 1, so $\frac{4}{8} < \frac{2}{3}$.

In third grade, children also learned these two facts about fractions:

- If the denominators are the same, the fraction with the greater numerator is greater because there are more parts that are the same size. Example: $\frac{3}{5} > \frac{1}{5}$.

- If the numerators are the same, the fraction with the *smaller* denominator is *greater*, because there are the same number of parts but the parts are smaller when the denominators is greater. Example: $\frac{2}{3} > \frac{2}{4}$ because fourths are smaller than thirds.

In fourth grade, children can use these facts to compare fractions by finding equivalent fractions that have the same numerator or same denominator. For example, to compare $\frac{4}{8}$ and $\frac{2}{3}$, you can multiply $\frac{2}{3}$ by $\frac{2}{2}$ to find an equivalent fraction with 4 as the numerator: $\frac{2\times2}{3\times2}=\frac{4}{6}$. Now, compare $\frac{4}{8}$ and $\frac{4}{6}$. Because $\frac{4}{8}$ has a greater denominator, it is the smaller fraction: $\frac{4}{8}<\frac{4}{6}$, so $\frac{4}{8}<\frac{2}{3}$.

Finding similar denominators to compare $\frac{4}{8}$ and $\frac{2}{3}$ takes two steps, because the first multiple that 3 and 8 have in common is 24. To find equivalent fractions with 24 as the denominator, multiply $\frac{4\times3}{8\times3}=\frac{12}{24}$ and $\frac{2\times8}{3\times8}=\frac{16}{24}$. Now, the fraction with the greater numerator is greater: $\frac{12}{24}<\frac{16}{24}$, so $\frac{4}{8}<\frac{2}{3}$.

As you work with your child, remind her that as a mathematician, she is expected to not only find answers, but be able to explain her work in several different ways so that other people can understand it.

? Quiz

1. Which number in place of the square would make the number sentence true?

$$\frac{1}{2}>\frac{\square}{4}$$

A. 1   B. 2   C. 3   D. 4

2. Use **estimation** to place each of the fractions below on the number line. Think about whether each fraction is close to 0, $\frac{1}{2}$, or 1.

$$\frac{4}{5},\frac{3}{3},\frac{2}{8},\frac{5}{12}$$

0 ├——————————————————————————————————┤ 1

Write an inequality to compare all four fractions.

3. Use common denominators to compare these fractions. Show your work.

$$\frac{2}{3} \underline{\hspace{1cm}} \frac{7}{12}$$

4. Use common numerators to compare these fractions. Show your work.

$$\frac{3}{4} \underline{\hspace{1cm}} \frac{6}{10}$$

5. Use <, >, or = to make each number sentence true. For each comparison, show two ways to prove that your answer is correct.

a) $\frac{1}{3} \underline{\hspace{1cm}} \frac{1}{2}$ b) $\frac{6}{10} \underline{\hspace{1cm}} \frac{4}{12}$ c) $\frac{9}{12} \underline{\hspace{1cm}} \frac{2}{8}$

✓ **Answers**

1. Which number in place of the square would make the number sentence true?

$$\frac{1}{2} > \frac{\square}{4}$$

A. 1   *B. 2*   *C. 3*   *D. 4*

The correct answer is A.

This problem can be solved by noticing that the denominator in $\frac{\square}{4}$ is larger than the denominator in $\frac{1}{2}$, so if the same numerator, 1, is used, the fraction that results, $\frac{1}{4}$ will be smaller. This question is a review of 3rd grade skills, addressing the idea that if the numerators are the same, a fraction with a greater denominator will be smaller. This is foundational to the 4th grade skill of finding equivalent fractions that allow the numerators and denominators to be compared.

2. Use **estimation** *to place each of the fractions below on the number line. Think about whether each fraction is close to 0, $\frac{1}{2}$, or 1.*

0 ————————————————— 1	$\frac{4}{5}, \frac{3}{3}, \frac{2}{8}, \frac{5}{12}$

Write an inequality to compare all four fractions.

The correct answer is:

$$\frac{2}{8} < \frac{5}{12} < \frac{4}{5} < \frac{3}{3}$$

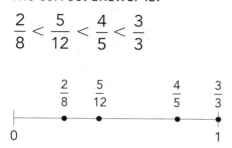

Use benchmark fractions to estimate each fraction's value. In the fraction $\frac{4}{5}$, the denominator is only a little bit greater than the numerator, so it is close to 1. In the fraction $\frac{3}{3}$, the numerator is equal to the denominator, so it is equal to 1. In the fraction $\frac{2}{8}$, the denominator is much greater than the numerator, so it is close to 0. In the fraction $\frac{5}{12}$, the denominator is about 2 times the numerator ($2 \times 6 = 12$), so the fraction is close to $\frac{1}{2}$. This means the fractions in order from least to greatest are $\frac{2}{8}$, $\frac{5}{12}$, $\frac{4}{5}$, and $\frac{3}{3}$, which can be written as the inequality $\frac{2}{8} < \frac{5}{12} < \frac{4}{5} < \frac{3}{3}$.

It is important for students to be able to estimate the value of fractions. This question gets them thinking about the approximate value of a fraction based on its similarity to the benchmark fractions 0, $\frac{1}{2}$, and 1 by comparing the value of the numerator to the value of the denominator.

3. Use common denominators to compare these fractions. Show your work.

$$\frac{2}{3} \underline{\quad\quad} \frac{7}{12}$$

The correct answer is >.

To compare using common denominators, the fractions must be written with the same denominator. The first multiple that 3 and 12 have in common is 12. To find a fraction equivalent to $\frac{2}{3}$ with 12 as a denominator, multiply $\frac{2}{3} \times \frac{4}{4} = \frac{8}{12}$. Now, the fraction with greater numerator is greater: $8 > 7$, so $\frac{2}{3} > \frac{7}{12}$.

This question is a bridge between the 3rd grade skill of addressing the idea that if the denominators are the same, a fraction with a greater numerator will be greater, and the 4th grade skill of finding equivalent fractions that allow the numerators and denominators to be compared.

4. Use common numerators to compare these fractions. Show your work.

$$\frac{3}{4} \underline{} \frac{6}{10}$$

The correct answer is >.

To compare using common numerators, the fractions must be written with the same numerator. The first multiple that 3 and 6 have in common is 6. To find a fraction equivalent to $\frac{3}{4}$ with 6 as a numerator, multiply $\frac{3}{4} \times \frac{2}{2} = \frac{6}{8}$. Now, the fraction with the smaller denominator is greater: $8 < 10$, so $\frac{3}{4} > \frac{6}{10}$.

This question is a bridge between the 3rd grade skill of addressing the idea that if the numerators are the same, a fraction with a greater denominator will be smaller, and the 4th grade skill of finding equivalent fractions that allow the numerators and denominators to be compared.

5. Use $<$, $>$, or $=$ to make each number sentence true. For each comparison, show two ways to prove that your answer is correct.

a) $\frac{1}{3} \underline{} \frac{1}{2}$ b) $\frac{6}{10} \underline{} \frac{4}{12}$ c) $\frac{9}{12} \underline{} \frac{2}{8}$

The correct answers are $<$, $>$, $>$.

For a, the fractions share the same numerator, so the one with the greater denominator, $\frac{1}{3}$ is less. Bar models can be used to check the relative sizes of the fractions.

For b, using a benchmark of $\frac{1}{2}$, notice that $6/10 > \frac{1}{2}$ because $5/10 = \frac{1}{2}$ and $4/12 < \frac{1}{2}$ because $6/12 = \frac{1}{2}$. To find a common numerator, notice that 6 and 4 are both factors of 12, so find equivalent fractions with 12 in the numerator: $\frac{6 \times 2}{10 \times 2} = \frac{12}{20}$ and $\frac{4 \times 3}{12 \times 3} = \frac{12}{36}$. Comparing these fractions shows that $\frac{12}{20} > \frac{12}{36}$.

For c, both fractions can be reduced so that the denominator is 4: $\frac{9 \div 3}{12 \div 3} = \frac{3}{4}$ and $\frac{2 \div 2}{8 \div 2} = \frac{1}{4}$. Now, compare: $\frac{3}{4} > \frac{1}{4}$. Using estimated or actual values on a number line, it can be seen that $\frac{9}{12}$ (which has a numerator that is close to the denominator) is to the right of $\frac{2}{8}$ (which has a numerator that is a lot less than the denominator).

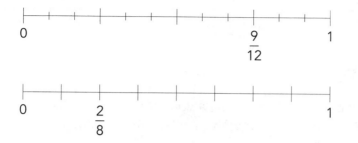

This question gives your child the chance to solve a basic comparison problem using a strategy of his or her choice. Your child might solve it using bar models or a number line, by comparing common numerators or denominators, or using benchmark fractions. This question is testing your child's ability to determine the best strategy to use depending on the fractions presented in the problem. It is also intended to test his or her ability to explain his or her reasoning so that others can understand it.

THE STANDARD

4.NF.B.3: *Understand a fraction a/b with a > 1 as a sum of fractions 1/b.*

4.NF.B.3a: *Understand addition and subtraction of fractions as joining and separating parts referring to the same whole.*

4.NF.B.3b: *Decompose a fraction into a sum of fractions with the same denominator in more than one way, recording each decomposition by an equation. Justify decompositions, e.g., by using a visual fraction model. Examples:* $\frac{3}{8}=\frac{1}{8}+\frac{1}{8}+\frac{1}{8}$; $\frac{3}{8}=\frac{1}{8}+\frac{2}{8}$; $2\frac{1}{8}=1+1+\frac{1}{8}=\frac{8}{8}+\frac{8}{8}+\frac{1}{8}$.

4.NF.B.3d: *Solve word problems involving addition and subtraction of fractions referring to the same whole and having like denominators, e.g., by using visual fraction models and equations to represent the problem.*

What does it mean?

This group of standards addresses adding fractions with like denominators. Students use the visual models developed earlier to understand any fraction as a combination of other fractions and then extend this to the procedure of adding fractions. At this level, denominators of fractions are limited to 2, 3, 4, 5, 6, 8, 10, 12, and 100.

Try this together

Your child should begin to understand adding and subtracting fractions through visual models.

This number line model shows how fractions with a numerator of 1, like $\frac{1}{8}$, can be added together to make fractions with larger numerators. $\frac{1}{8}+\frac{1}{8}+\frac{1}{8}+\frac{1}{8}+\frac{1}{8}+\frac{1}{8}=\frac{6}{8}$. Your child should also be familiar decomposing fractions, or breaking them up into parts: $\frac{6}{8}=\frac{1}{8}+\frac{1}{8}+\frac{1}{8}+\frac{1}{8}+\frac{1}{8}+\frac{1}{8}$.

Fractions can be decomposed in more than one way. For example, $\frac{6}{8}=\frac{4}{8}+\frac{2}{8}$.

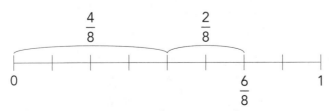

This idea of decomposition can also be represented using a bar model. The model below shows that $\frac{5}{10} = \frac{1}{10} + \frac{4}{10}$. Notice that the whole bar is divided into 10 equal parts because the denominator is 10.

Subtraction is thought of as removing parts instead of combining them. So the difference $\frac{5}{6} - \frac{2}{6}$ can be viewed as starting with 5 parts that are each $\frac{1}{6}$ and taking 2 parts away. $\frac{5}{6} - \frac{2}{6} = \frac{3}{6}$.

In fourth grade, your child will only see sums (adding) and differences (subtracting) with fractions that have the same denominator. Because the parts are always the same size, the sum can be found by adding the numerators and the difference can be found by subtracting the numerators.

However, it is important to keep these procedures linked to mathematical models so that your child understands why he cannot add or subtract fractions with different denominators using the same strategy: $\frac{2}{3} + \frac{4}{5}$ does not equal $\frac{6}{8}$!

? Quiz

1. Find two ways to write the fraction $\frac{3}{4}$ as a sum of other fractions with a denominator of four. Draw number lines or bar models to show your thinking.

2. Which fraction is equal to $\frac{5}{12} + \frac{3}{12}$?

   A. $\frac{2}{12}$ B. $\frac{8}{12}$ C. $\frac{6}{12}$ D. $\frac{15}{12}$

3. What number in place of the square makes the number sentence true?

$$\frac{8}{10} - \frac{\square}{10} = \frac{2}{10}$$

   A. 10   B. 1   C. 6   D. 4

4. Kristen and Amy share a birthday cake. Kristen ate $\frac{3}{8}$ of the cake and Amy ate $\frac{2}{8}$ of the cake. How much of the cake did they eat together? Show your work using a number line.

5. Frank's mom is using one sheet of wrapping paper to wrap two presents. If the first present uses $\frac{1}{5}$ of the paper and the second uses $\frac{2}{5}$ of the paper, then how much of the paper is left? Show your work using a bar model.

 **Answers**

1. Find two ways to write the fraction $\frac{3}{4}$ as a sum of other fractions with a denominator of 4. Draw number lines or bar models to show your thinking.

The correct answers are: $\frac{1}{4} + \frac{2}{4}$ and $\frac{1}{4} + \frac{1}{4} + \frac{1}{4}$.

To create the fractions, first start by drawing $\frac{3}{4}$ and then look for different ways to break up the 3 fourths. Being able to decompose fractions makes it easier for students to understand the "why" of adding fractions. Questions such as this one support understanding that there are many possible decompositions. As you work with your child on this type of problem using fractions with greater numerators, help her to find as many combinations as possible.

2. Which fraction is equal to $\dfrac{5}{12} + \dfrac{3}{12}$?

   A. $\dfrac{2}{12}$ B. $\dfrac{8}{12}$ C. $\dfrac{6}{12}$ D. $\dfrac{15}{12}$

   The correct answer is B.

   $$\frac{5}{12} + \frac{3}{12} = \frac{5+3}{12} = \frac{8}{12}$$

   This question is one of the skills-based questions your child may see, which assess whether he can apply the appropriate procedures and find the correct answer. When solving these, any type of method is acceptable, and asking your child to justify the answer with several methods can support understanding.

3. What number in place of the square makes the number sentence true?

   $$\frac{8}{10} - \frac{\square}{10} = \frac{2}{10}$$

   A. 10   B. 1   C. 6   D. 4

   The correct answer is C.

   The best approach to this problem is to focus on the numerators. To get 2, something was subtracted from 8. This must be 6 because 8 − 6 = 2. This can also be seen with a bar model "how much must we take away from $\dfrac{8}{10}$ to get $\dfrac{2}{10}$?" This question requires your child to think about subtraction in a less typical format. She is given the result of the subtraction, and must understand how each of the numbers works together in the equation. When working with questions like these, visual models are very helpful.

4. Kristen and Amy share a birthday cake. Kristen ate $\dfrac{3}{8}$ of the cake and Amy ate $\dfrac{2}{8}$ of the cake. How much of the cake did they eat together? Show your work using a number line.

   The correct answer is $\dfrac{5}{8}$ and a number line model like this one:

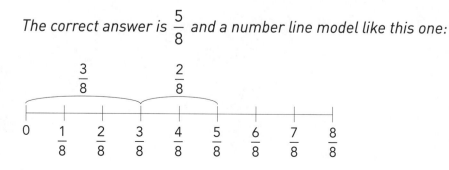

To solve by adding, take $\frac{3}{8} + \frac{2}{8} = \frac{(3+2)}{8} = \frac{5}{8}$. *This question requires your child to use skills he has acquired from solving word problems with whole numbers, such as noticing clues like ate, together, uses, and left to apply the correct operation. They also require your child to justify his thinking using a model without any references, so that he takes more command of his learning. Question 5 adds another layer of challenge in recalling that a whole sheet of wrapping paper is equivalent to* $\frac{5}{5}$.

5. Frank's mom is using one sheet of wrapping paper to wrap two presents. If the first present uses $\frac{1}{5}$ of the paper and the second uses $\frac{2}{5}$ of the paper, then how much of the paper is left? Show your work using a bar model.

The correct answer is $\frac{2}{5}$ *and a bar model like this one:*

Because she starts with a whole sheet of wrapping paper, she begins with $\frac{5}{5}$. *She then subtracts* $\frac{1}{5}$ *and then* $\frac{2}{5}$ *to get* $\frac{5}{5} - \frac{2}{5} - \frac{1}{5} = \frac{2}{5}$. *This question requires your child to use skills he has acquired from solving word problems with whole numbers, such as noticing clues like ate, together, uses, and left to apply the correct operation. They also require your child to justify his thinking using a model without any references, so that he takes more command of his learning. Question 5 adds another layer of challenge in recalling that a whole sheet of wrapping paper is equivalent to* $\frac{5}{5}$.

THE STANDARD

4.NF.B.3a: *Understand addition and subtraction of fractions as joining and separating parts referring to the same whole.*

4.NF.B.3c: *Add and subtract mixed numbers with like denominators, e.g., by replacing each mixed number with an equivalent fraction, and/or by using properties of operations and the relationship between addition and subtraction.*

4.NF.B.3d: *Solve word problems involving addition and subtraction of fractions referring to the same whole and having like denominators, e.g., by using visual fraction models and equations to represent the problem.*

What does it mean?

The set of standards studied in the previous lesson also apply to fractions with numerators larger than the denominator. This type of fraction can be written as an improper fraction or a mixed number, and students should be able to move between the formats to solve problems. At this level, denominators of fractions are limited to 2, 3, 4, 5, 6, 8, 10, 12, and 100.

Try this together

In the 4th grade, students continue their exploration of mixed numbers, which are composed of a whole number and a fractional part. As before, bar models and number line models are used to develop the conceptual understanding of mixed numbers.

For example, the mixed number $2\frac{1}{3}$ can be represented by 2 wholes and then another $\frac{1}{3}$ of a whole.

Your child should understand that each whole bar represents 1 whole, and that this is equivalent to $\frac{3}{3}$. (In general, any fraction with the same numerator and denominator equals 1.) Then, your child can use decomposition strategies from lesson 7 to rewrite the fraction in different ways: $2\frac{1}{3}=1+1+\frac{1}{3}$ or $2\frac{1}{3}=\frac{3}{3}+\frac{3}{3}+\frac{1}{3}=\frac{3+3+1}{3}=\frac{7}{3}$. Being able to decompose the fraction in different ways is critical to success in adding and subtracting.

A **mixed number** is written as a whole number and a fraction in lowest terms $\left(2\frac{1}{3}\right)$ while an **improper fraction** has no whole number, and the numerator is larger than the denominator $\left(\frac{7}{3}\right)$. The number can also be decomposed in other ways that only convert some of the wholes into fractional parts. For example, $2\frac{1}{3} = 1 + 1 + \frac{1}{3} = 1 + \frac{3}{3} + \frac{1}{3} = 1\frac{4}{3}$.

When adding or subtracting these mixed numbers, there are two approaches that your child may use, and she should be familiar with both. The first involves converting all mixed numbers completely into improper fractions:

To add $3\frac{1}{2} + 1\frac{1}{2}$, find the improper fraction that is equivalent to each number: $3\frac{1}{2} = 1+1+1+\frac{1}{2} = \frac{2}{2} + \frac{2}{2} + \frac{2}{2} + \frac{1}{2} = \frac{7}{2}$, and $1\frac{1}{2} = 1 + \frac{1}{2} = \frac{2}{2} + \frac{1}{2} = \frac{3}{2}$.

Then, add the fractions by keeping the denominators (size of each part) the same and adding the numerators (number of parts selected): $\frac{7}{2} + \frac{3}{2} = \frac{10}{2}$. Finally, reduce to lowest terms: $\frac{10 \div 2}{2 \div 2} = \frac{5}{1} = 5$.

The other strategy involves keeping as much of the number as possible set up as a whole number, and then regrouping if necessary. Several examples are shown below.

This example does not require any regrouping:

$$5\frac{2}{3} - 2\frac{1}{3} = 5 + \frac{2}{3} - 2 - \frac{1}{3} = 5 - 2 + \frac{2}{3} - \frac{1}{3} = 3 + \frac{1}{3} = 3\frac{1}{3}$$

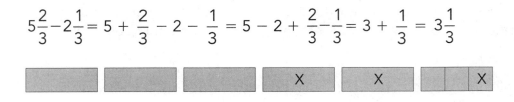

In addition, regrouping fractional parts into whole numbers may occur after the fractional parts are added:

$$2\frac{3}{4} + 1\frac{2}{4} = 2 + 1 + \frac{3}{4} + \frac{2}{4} = 2 + 1 + \frac{5}{4} = 2 + 1 + \frac{4}{4} + \frac{1}{4} = 2 + 1 + 1 + \frac{1}{4} = 4 + \frac{1}{4} = 4\frac{1}{4}$$

In subtraction, if the fractional part of the second number is greater than the fractional part of the first, one of the wholes from the first number must be regrouped into a fraction:

$$2\frac{2}{6} - 1\frac{5}{6} = 1 + 1 + \frac{2}{6} - 1 - \frac{5}{6} = 1 + \frac{6}{6} + \frac{2}{6} - 1 - \frac{5}{6} = 1 + \frac{8}{6} - 1 - 5/6 = 1 - 1 +$$

$$\frac{8}{6} - \frac{5}{6} = 0 + \frac{3}{6} = \frac{3}{6}$$

When working with mixed numbers, be sure to always refer back to the visual models. Your child will need to be able to understand what they represent both to explain his thinking in 4th grade and to support advanced fraction work in 5th grade.

? Quiz

1. Which of the following is equivalent to $\frac{6}{8} + \frac{3}{8}$?

   A. $9\frac{1}{8}$ B. $11\frac{9}{8}$ C. $1\frac{1}{8}$ D. $8\frac{1}{9}$

2. Which of the following is equivalent to $3\frac{2}{12} - 2\frac{11}{12}$?

   A. $\frac{3}{12}$ B. $\frac{4}{12}$ C. $\frac{9}{12}$ D. $\frac{15}{12}$

3. Which number in place of the square makes the number sentence true?

   $$10\frac{3}{10} + \square = 14\frac{5}{10}$$

   A. $4\frac{2}{10}$ B. $3\frac{5}{10}$ C. $4\frac{8}{10}$ D. $3\frac{7}{10}$

4. Samantha is building a piece of furniture and will need one piece of wood that is $4\frac{6}{8}$ feet long and another that is $2\frac{3}{8}$ feet long. How many total feet of wood will she need? Show your work with equations and a bar model.

5. Jake's toy had $6\frac{1}{3}$ inches of string attached to it. He then cut $2\frac{2}{3}$ inches of the string off. How many inches of string are still attached to the toy? Show your work with equations and a bar model.

Answers

1. Which of the following is equivalent to $\frac{6}{8}+\frac{3}{8}$?

A. $9\frac{1}{8}$ B. $11\frac{9}{8}$ C. $1\frac{1}{8}$ D. $8\frac{1}{9}$

The correct answer is C.

$$\frac{6}{8}+\frac{3}{8}=\frac{9}{8}=\frac{8}{8}+\frac{1}{8}=1+\frac{1}{8}=1\frac{1}{8}$$

This question reviews basic fraction addition and regrouping the improper fraction in the answer to make a mixed number.

2. Which of the following is equivalent to $3\frac{2}{12}-2\frac{11}{12}$?

A. $\frac{3}{12}$ B. $\frac{4}{12}$ C. $\frac{9}{12}$ D. $\frac{15}{12}$

The correct answer is A.
Because the fractional part of the second number is greater than the fractional part of the first number, one of the wholes of the first number must be regrouped into a fraction.

$$3\frac{2}{12} - 2\frac{11}{12} = 2\frac{14}{12} - 2\frac{11}{12} = \frac{3}{12}$$

This question asks students to identify a situation where regrouping is necessary. Although this problem can be solved by converting to improper fractions, the size of the numerators is so large that there is a chance of making a sloppy arithmetic error, so working with whole numbers as much as possible is recommended. You should practice conversions like these with your child using visual models as a guide.

3. Which number in place of the square makes the number sentence true?

$$10\frac{3}{10} + \square = 14\frac{5}{10}$$

A. $4\frac{2}{10}$ B. $3\frac{5}{10}$ C. $4\frac{8}{10}$ D. $3\frac{7}{10}$

The correct answer is A.

Looking at the fractional parts, 2 tenths are needed to reach $\frac{5}{10}$. Then, looking at the wholes, 4 wholes are needed to reach 14. This question encourages your child to think algebraically in the setting of mixed numbers. Noticing that 2 tenths and 4 wholes are needed helps your child think about the values of wholes and fractional parts.

4. Samantha is building a piece of furniture and will need one piece of wood that is $4\frac{6}{8}$ feet long and another that is $2\frac{3}{8}$ feet long. How many total feet of wood will she need?

The correct answer is $7\frac{1}{8}$.

Because the question asks for the total, the two mixed numbers should be added. Because adding the two fractional parts will result in an improper fraction, the new fractional part must be regrouped into a whole number.

$$4\frac{6}{8} + 2\frac{3}{8} = 4 + 2 + \frac{6}{8} + \frac{3}{8} = 4 + 2 + \frac{9}{8} = 4 + 2 + \frac{8}{8} + \frac{1}{8} = 4 + 2 + 1 + \frac{1}{8} =$$
$$7 + \frac{1}{8} = 7\frac{1}{8}$$

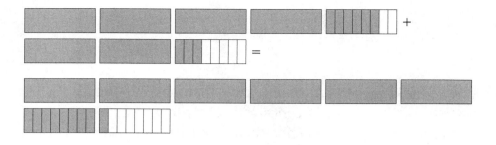

This question, like the question that follows, is an example of the types of word problems that your child may see under this standard. These test their ability to recognize which operation to use and their ability in applying that operation to mixed numbers. Requiring visual models and equations allows your child to justify his answer in a way that others can understand—and can also give you, his teachers, and himself insights into his learning. Question 4 addresses addition with regrouping and question 5 addresses subtraction with regrouping, which are the most challenging skills under these standards.

5. Jake's toy had $6\frac{1}{3}$ inches of string attached to it. He then cut $2\frac{2}{3}$ inches of the string off. How many inches of string are still attached to the toy?

The correct answer is $3\frac{2}{3}$.

Because Jake removes string from the toy, the amount he removes should be subtracted from the original length. Because the fractional part of the second number is greater than the fractional part of the first number, one of the wholes of the first number must be regrouped into a fraction.

THE STANDARD

4.NF.B.4: *Apply and extend previous understandings of multiplication to multiply a fraction by a whole number.*

4.NF.B.4a: *Understand a fraction $\frac{a}{b}$ as a multiple of $\frac{1}{b}$. For example, use a visual fraction model to represent $\frac{5}{4}$ as the product $5 \times \left(\frac{1}{4}\right)$, recording the conclusion by the equation $\frac{5}{4} = 5 \times \left(\frac{1}{4}\right)$.*

What does it mean?

Using visual fraction models and their understanding of multiplication as repeated addition, students are expected to be able to take any fraction and represent is as the result of multiplying a whole number and a unit fraction. This decomposition is later used to understand whole number and fraction multiplication in general. At this level, denominators of fractions are limited to 2, 3, 4, 5, 6, 8, 10, 12, and 100.

Try this together

When students were first introduced to multiplication, they saw the idea of multiplication as repeated addition. For example, 5×4 is thought of as 4 added to itself 5 times: $4 + 4 + 4 + 4 + 4$.

When working with fractions, this idea can be used to see how any fraction can be written as a product. This skill combines your child's ability to represent a fraction with visual models like number lines or bar models with their ability to write a fraction as a sum of other fractions. Your child has already studied how to take a fraction like $\frac{8}{10}$ and, using a number line, represent it as $\frac{1}{10} + \frac{1}{10} + \frac{1}{10} + \frac{1}{10} + \frac{1}{10} + \frac{1}{10} + \frac{1}{10} + \frac{1}{10}$.

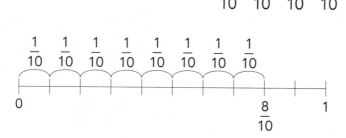

Now, they should be able to state that $\frac{1}{10}+\frac{1}{10}+\frac{1}{10}+\frac{1}{10}+\frac{1}{10}+\frac{1}{10}+\frac{1}{10}+\frac{1}{10}=8\times\frac{1}{10}$ and therefore $\frac{8}{10}=8\times\frac{1}{10}$. This also relates back to their understanding of a fraction as the number of parts of a whole. The fraction $\frac{8}{10}$, or eight tenths, represents a total of 8 pieces of a whole that is divided into 10 equal size pieces.

Similarly, looking at the bar model for $\frac{6}{5}$, it can be seen that this fraction is

$\frac{1}{5}+\frac{1}{5}+\frac{1}{5}+\frac{1}{5}+\frac{1}{5}+\frac{1}{5}$ or $6\times\frac{1}{5}$.

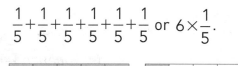

In general, any fraction $\frac{a}{b}$ where a and b are nonzero can be written as $a\times\frac{1}{b}$. While it is possible for your child to simply memorize this rule, working with the models helps provide a deeper understanding of why the rule is true.

Finally, this strategy can be applied to calculating any product of the form $a\times\frac{1}{b}$. For example, to find the product $3\times\frac{1}{2}$, use a visual model to see that $3\times\frac{1}{2}=\frac{1}{2}+\frac{1}{2}+\frac{1}{2}=\frac{1+1+1}{2}=\frac{3}{2}$ or apply the rule stated above.

? Quiz

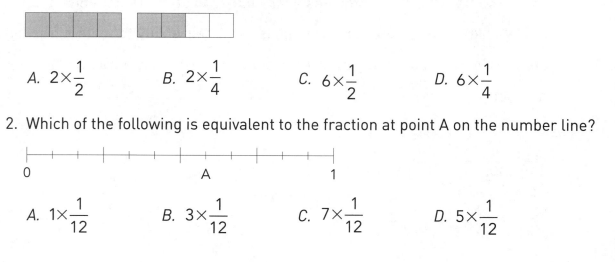

1. Which of the following is equivalent to the fraction represented by the bar model?

    A. $2\times\frac{1}{2}$ B. $2\times\frac{1}{4}$ C. $6\times\frac{1}{2}$ D. $6\times\frac{1}{4}$

2. Which of the following is equivalent to the fraction at point A on the number line?

    A. $1\times\frac{1}{12}$ B. $3\times\frac{1}{12}$ C. $7\times\frac{1}{12}$ D. $5\times\frac{1}{12}$

3. Which of the following is equal to $10 \times \frac{1}{2}$?

A. $\frac{9}{2}$ B. $\frac{10}{2}$ C. $\frac{11}{2}$ D. $\frac{20}{2}$

4. For each of the fractions below, write an equivalent expression that is the product of a whole number and a fraction.

a) $\frac{17}{4} = $ ____ $\times$ ____   b) $\frac{8}{12} = $ ____ $\times$ ____

5. LaTaja needs $3\frac{1}{2}$ cups of flour for her bread recipe. She does not have a 1-cup measure so she can only use a $\frac{1}{2}$-cup measure. She sets up the equation below.

$$\underline{\quad} \times \frac{1}{2} = 3\frac{1}{2}$$

Find the number that goes in the blank and then explain what it means in LaTaja's situation.

✓ Answers

1. Which of the following is equivalent to the fraction represented by the bar model?

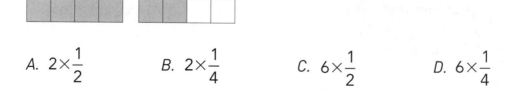

A. $2 \times \frac{1}{2}$ B. $2 \times \frac{1}{4}$ C. $6 \times \frac{1}{2}$ D. $6 \times \frac{1}{4}$

The correct answer is D. Each "whole" of the bar model is divided into 4 equal pieces.

Counting, there are a total of 6 of these. Therefore, the fraction can be viewed as $6 \times \frac{1}{4}$.

Questions 1 and 2 are designed to test your child's ability to take a visual model and apply the conceptual meaning behind writing fractions as products of whole numbers and unit fractions. These types of questions are deeper than simply "finding the product" and sup-port a more comprehensive understanding of multiplication.

2. Which of the following is equivalent to the fraction at point A on the number line?

A. $1 \times \dfrac{1}{12}$ B. $3 \times \dfrac{1}{12}$ C. $7 \times \dfrac{1}{12}$ D. $5 \times \dfrac{1}{12}$

The correct answer is C.

The number line is evenly divided into 12 pieces, therefore the fraction at point A is $\dfrac{7}{12}$ which is equivalent to $7 \times \dfrac{1}{12}$.

3. Which of the following is equal to $10 \times \dfrac{1}{2}$?

A. $\dfrac{9}{2}$ B. $\dfrac{10}{2}$ C. $\dfrac{11}{2}$ D. $\dfrac{20}{2}$

The correct answer is B.

Using the general rule, $10 \times \dfrac{1}{2} = \dfrac{10 \times 1}{2} = \dfrac{10}{2}$. Questions 3 and 4 assess your child's under-standing of the general rule that $a \times \dfrac{1}{b} = \dfrac{a}{b}$. Your child should be able to easily apply the rule and explain why it works using models and words.

4. For each of the fractions below, write an equivalent expression that is the product of a whole number and a fraction.

a) $\dfrac{17}{4} = $ _____ × _____

b) $\dfrac{8}{12} = $ _____ × _____

The correct answers are $17 \times \dfrac{1}{4}$ and $8 \times \dfrac{1}{12}$.

The fraction $\dfrac{a}{b}$ where a and b are nonzero can always be written as $a \times \dfrac{1}{b}$. For part a, a = 17 and b = 4. For part b, a = 8 and b = 12.

5. LaTaja needs $3\frac{1}{2}$ cups of flour for her bread recipe. She does not have a 1-cup measure so she can only use a $\frac{1}{2}$-cup measure. She sets up the equation below.

$$\underline{\quad} \times \frac{1}{2} = 3\frac{1}{2}$$

Find the number that goes in the blank and then explain what it means in LaTaja's situation.

The correct answer is 7 and an explanation that 7 is the number of times that LaTaja will need to use the $\frac{1}{2}$ cup measure.

The first step in this problem is to convert the mixed number, $3\frac{1}{2}$, to an improper fraction:
$$3\frac{1}{2} = 1 + 1 + 1 + \frac{1}{2} = \frac{2}{2} + \frac{2}{2} + \frac{2}{2} + \frac{1}{2} = \frac{7}{2}.$$

Now, the problem looks more familiar: if $\underline{\quad} \times \frac{1}{2} = \frac{7}{2}$, then the unknown number is 7.

In this problem, 7 represents the number of times that LaTaja should use the $\frac{1}{2}$-cup measure to get $\frac{7}{2}$ or $3\frac{1}{2}$ cups of flour.

Question 5 is a challenging question for two reasons. First, it begins with a mixed number which your child must realize should be converted to an improper fraction. Second, it uses a context and requires your child to understand the use of the number in the context. Questions like this are ultimately the type of problems that your child should be comfortable solving using the skills developed in the more basic practice.

 # THE STANDARD

4.NF.B.4b: *Understand a multiple of $\dfrac{a}{b}$ as a multiple of $\dfrac{1}{b}$, and use this understanding to multiply a fraction by a whole number. For example, use a visual fraction model to express $3 \times \left(\dfrac{2}{5} \right)$ as $6 \times \left(\dfrac{1}{5} \right)$, recognizing this product as $\dfrac{6}{5}$. (In general, $n \times \left(\dfrac{a}{b} \right) = \dfrac{(n \times a)}{b}$.)*

4.NF.B.4c: *Solve word problems involving multiplication of a fraction by a whole number, e.g., by using visual fraction models and equations to represent the problem. For example, if each person at a party will eat $\dfrac{3}{8}$ of a pound of roast beef, and there will be 5 people at the party, how many pounds of roast beef will be needed? Between what two whole numbers does your answer lie?*

What does it mean?

Students are expected to be able to find the product of a whole number and any fraction. This skill may be applied in many settings including with word problems. As with all fraction based standards, visual models are heavily used. At this level, denominators of fractions are limited to 2, 3, 4, 5, 6, 8, 10, 12, and 100.

Try this together

Prior to working with problems under this standard, your child will have used bar models and number line models to understand how to find the product of a whole number and a unit fraction. Using these same methods, your child will be introduced to multiplying whole numbers and any general fraction.

To illustrate this, let's take a look at the product $3 \times \dfrac{2}{8}$. Using their understanding of multiplication, your child should be able to write this product as $\dfrac{2}{8} + \dfrac{2}{8} + \dfrac{2}{8}$ and then represent this using a visual model such as a number line.

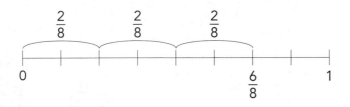

Based on this model, $3 \times \dfrac{2}{8} = \dfrac{6}{8}$, but looking a bit closer can illustrate a more general method.

$\dfrac{2}{8}$ $\qquad$ $\dfrac{2}{8}$ $\qquad$ $\dfrac{2}{8}$

0 $\quad$ $\dfrac{1}{8}$ $\quad$ $\dfrac{1}{8}$ $\quad$ $\dfrac{1}{8}$ $\quad$ $\dfrac{1}{8}$ $\quad$ $\dfrac{1}{8}$ $\quad$ $\dfrac{1}{8}$ $\dfrac{6}{8}$ $\qquad$ 1

This closer look shows that $3 \times \dfrac{2}{8} = 6 \times \dfrac{1}{8}$, which your child has learned is equivalent to $\dfrac{6}{8}$. The general rule is that for any product $a \times \dfrac{b}{c}$ where a, b, and c are nonzero, the product is $\dfrac{a \times b}{c}$.

This understanding can also be shown using a bar model. For example, to find $5 \times \dfrac{2}{4}$, start with $\dfrac{2}{4}$ repeated 5 times and count the number of fourths. This shows that $5 \times \dfrac{2}{4} = \dfrac{5 \times 2}{4} = \dfrac{10}{4}$.

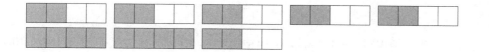

There are 10 shaded parts of the bar model, where each part represents a fourth. This is represented by the fraction $\dfrac{10}{4}$.

At this level, your child should memorize the general property and be able to apply it with models, in problems with numbers only, and in word problems. Your child should also be able to justify or explain why a multiplication equation is true. Regular use of these visual models reinforces the meaning behind the general rule.

❓ Quiz

1. Which of the following is equivalent to $4 \times \dfrac{3}{8}$?

   A. $7 \times \dfrac{1}{8}$ $\qquad$ B. $1 \times \dfrac{1}{8}$ $\qquad$ C. $12 \times \dfrac{1}{8}$ $\qquad$ D. $32 \times \dfrac{1}{8}$

2. Which of the following is equivalent to $14 \times \dfrac{1}{5}$?

   A. $7 \times \dfrac{7}{5}$ $\qquad$ B. $2 \times \dfrac{12}{5}$ $\qquad$ C. $10 \times \dfrac{4}{5}$ $\qquad$ D. $2 \times \dfrac{7}{5}$

3. What is the product of 2 and $\frac{5}{6}$?

A. $\frac{10}{6}$ B. $\frac{7}{6}$ C. $\frac{5}{8}$ D. $\frac{5}{12}$

4. Mr. Hayes is baking cookies for his family. The recipe calls for $\frac{3}{4}$ cup of sugar. If he wants to make 5 times as much as the recipe, how many cups of sugar should he use?

5. Margaret is decorating a board for a party. She tapes one balloon to the board every $\frac{2}{3}$ feet, and the board is $4\frac{2}{3}$ feet long. She writes the equation below:

$$\underline{\quad} \times \frac{2}{3} \text{ feet} = 4\frac{2}{3} \text{ feet}$$

Fill in the missing number and explain what it means for Margaret's situation.

☑ **Answers**

1. Which of the following is equivalent to $4 \times \frac{3}{8}$?

A. $7 \times \frac{1}{8}$ B. $1 \times \frac{1}{8}$ C. $12 \times \frac{1}{8}$ D. $32 \times \frac{1}{8}$

The correct answer is C.

Using the general rule, $4 \times \frac{3}{8} = \frac{4 \times 3}{8} = \frac{12}{8}$. However, any fraction can be written as the product of a whole number and a unit fraction, so $\frac{12}{8} = 12 \times \frac{1}{8}$.

Questions 1 and 2 are focused on the skill of rewriting a product of a whole number and any fraction as the product of a whole number and a unit fraction. Being comfortable with going back and forth between these forms helps your child understand operations on a deeper level. To further assist with this, visual models should be used whenever possible.

2. Which of the following is equivalent to $14 \times \frac{1}{5}$?

   A. $7 \times \frac{7}{5}$ B. $2 \times \frac{12}{5}$ C. $10 \times \frac{4}{5}$ D. $2 \times \frac{7}{5}$

   The correct answer is D.

   There are several possible approaches to this question. One method which would be good for practice is to find the product $14 \times \frac{1}{5} = \frac{14}{5}$, and then compare it to the product from each answer choice. The only equivalent product is D.

3. What is the product of 2 and $\frac{5}{6}$?

   A. $\frac{10}{6}$ B. $\frac{7}{6}$ C. $\frac{5}{8}$ D. $\frac{5}{12}$

   The correct answer is A.

   Using the general rule, $2 \times \frac{5}{6} = \frac{2 \times 5}{6} = \frac{10}{6}$.

   Question 3 is a basic skills question which requires your child to apply the general rule to multiply the two values. Notice that the vocabulary is important. Your child should know that the word "product" implies "multiply."

4. Mr. Hayes is baking cookies for his family. The recipe calls for $\frac{3}{4}$ cup of sugar. If he wants to make 5 times as much as the recipe, how many cups of sugar should he use?

   The correct answer is $\frac{15}{4}$ or $3\frac{3}{4}$.

   Because he added the $\frac{3}{4}$ cup 5 times, the product of 5 and $\frac{3}{4}$ is needed to find the final answer. The final answer can be expressed as an improper fraction or a mixed number.

   $$5 \times \frac{3}{4} = \frac{5 \times 3}{4} = \frac{15}{4} = 3\frac{3}{4}$$

   Questions 4 and 5 show multiplication in the context of a real-life situation and require children to look for clues in solving it. Question 5 also focuses on the meaning of each of the numbers in the answer, and on going through several steps of converting a mixed number to an improper fraction and thinking of the missing factor instead of the product using decomposition. Solving word questions like these is one of the major goals of this standard, and is the level of understanding that all children should be comfortable with.

5. Margaret is decorating a wall for a party. She tapes one balloon to the wall every $\frac{2}{3}$ feet, and the wall is 8 feet long. She writes the equation below:

$$\underline{\quad} \times \frac{2}{3} \text{ feet} = 4\frac{2}{3} \text{ feet}$$

The correct answer is 7 and an explanation that Margaret will need 7 balloons.

The first step is to write $8\frac{2}{3}$ *as an improper fraction:* $4\frac{2}{3} = \frac{3}{3} + \frac{3}{3} + \frac{3}{3} + \frac{3}{3} + \frac{2}{3} = \frac{14}{3}.$

Then, use decomposition to think of $\frac{14}{3}$ *as 7 groups that are each equal to* $\frac{2}{3}$ *because* $2 \times 7 = 14.$

The equation shows that 7 balloons should be used every $\frac{2}{3}$ *feet to cover a total of* $4\frac{2}{3}$ *feet.*

ENGLISH LANGUAGE ARTS POST-TEST

The following questions are intended to assess your child's reading and writing skills. As with the pre-test, there are a variety of question types at various levels of cognition. These are typical of the types of questions that your fourth grader might experience in the classroom, as homework, and in assessment situations. These items are **not** designed to replicate standardized tests used to assess a child's reading level or a school's progress in helping the child achieve grade level.

A grid at the end provides the main Common Core standard assessed, as well as a brief explanation of the correct answers. This is intended to help you consider how your child is doing in reading and writing after you have presented the lessons in this book. Keep in mind, however, that building reading and writing skills is an ongoing process. The best way to build these skills is to continue to read and write. If the post-test identifies areas in which your child needs improvement, review the strategies in the lessons and continue to focus on these areas when you read with your child.

For each section, read the passage and then answer the questions that follow.

 School Lunches

School lunches are an important part of a student's day, and they should be considered as necessary as gym or math class. Lunch provides fuel for the brain and the body. It makes learning possible. This has been demonstrated time and again in many scientific studies.

This is why I was saddened to hear that budget cuts might mean that the school lunch program will suffer. Students who cannot afford to buy lunch at school should be provided with lunch free of cost, without exception. Students from poor families already have a disadvantage compared to other students. For example, poor students cannot afford tutors and additional study aids to help them with difficult subjects. Sometimes they have to work after school to earn money for their families, and this can hurt their ability to do homework. Why would school officials want to make it even harder for them to succeed?

Aside from the issue of free lunches, the school lunch program has another serious problem. The quality of the food offered to students is often unsatisfactory. Canned and cooked vegetables are used rather than fresh vegetables, which have more nutrients. On the rare occasion when fresh vegetables are offered, they are very popular. Because of this, the kitchen staff gives out smaller portions to make sure they do not run out. When they do this, students do not get the serving sizes that they are supposed to get. Higher quality food must be offered at the serving sizes recommended by experts.

Another problem with the lunch menu is its lack of choices. If every other Tuesday is "pork chop day," how does that affect Jewish and Muslim students? They cannot eat pork, so they must settle for eating side dishes instead. And what about vegetarians? There are many options that offer high protein without meat, such as beans. But beans are not usually on the menu. The limited menu can also pose a problem for students with medical restrictions, such as nut or gluten allergies.

All of these issues—free lunch cutbacks, poor quality, and lack of menu choices—are the result of a lack of money. In my opinion, school lunch programs should not be evaluated based on profit. They should be considered part of the overall cost of education. Do people ever complain about how much the math program costs? And yet, good nutrition is just as important to keep young minds sharp.

1. Which of the following sums up the main argument of this passage?
   A. *Poor students deserve the same educational opportunities as other students.*
   B. *School cafeteria workers should give out correct portion sizes.*
   C. *All students should have access to high-quality school lunches.*
   D. *Money should be the number-one concern for all school lunch programs.*

2. Based on its usage in the first paragraph, which of the following is closest in meaning to the word "demonstrated"?
   A. *refuted*   B. *proven*   C. *assisted*   D. *believed*

3. According to the passage, which of the following is an example of how the food quality is bad?
   A. *Students are given smaller serving sizes than they should be.*
   B. *Canned vegetables are offered instead of fresh vegetables.*
   C. *Students are not offered alternatives to meat.*
   D. *The lunch program budget was cut.*

4. Based on its usage in the second paragraph, which of the following is closest in meaning to the word "disadvantage"?
   A. *penalty*   B. *help*   C. *sympathy*   D. *scarcity*

5. Which of the following is given as an example of how poor students have a more difficult time than other students?
   A. *They have to eat low-quality food from the cafeteria.*
   B. *They are given smaller lunch portions than other students.*
   C. *They cannot afford tutors and additional study aids.*
   D. *They cannot participate in after-school activities that require expensive equipment.*

6. Based on its usage in the third paragraph, which of the following is closest in meaning to the word "unsatisfactory"?
   A. *factory made* B. *expensive*   C. *not proven*   D. *not good enough*

7. Which of the following best sums up the main idea of the fourth paragraph?
   A. *Students with medical restrictions are not always given good meal options.*
   B. *Vegetarians can still get protein by eating beans instead of meat.*
   C. *Jewish and Muslim students should not have to eat pork.*
   D. *Lunch menus should include options for different student lifestyles and needs.*

8. Based on this passage, what can you conclude is the major reason for problems with most lunch programs?

   _____

   _____

9. Based on its usage in the third paragraph, which of the following is closest in meaning to the word "evaluated"?

   A. judged   *B. spent*   *C. eliminated*   *D. admired*

10. According to the author, why is lunch in school important?

   _____

   _____

A Little Princess by Frances Hodgson Burnett (excerpt)

Once on a dark winter's day, when the yellow fog hung so thick and heavy in the streets of London that the lamps were lighted and the shop windows blazed with gas as they do at night, an odd-looking little girl sat in a cab with her father and was driven rather slowly through the big thoroughfares.

She sat with her feet tucked under her, and leaned against her father, who held her in his arm, as she stared out of the window at the passing people with a queer old-fashioned thoughtfulness in her big eyes.

She was such a little girl that one did not expect to see such a look on her small face. It would have been an old look for a child of twelve, and Sara Crewe was only seven. The fact was, however, that she was always dreaming and thinking odd things and could not herself remember any time when she had not been thinking things about grown-up people and the world they belonged to. She felt as if she had lived a long, long time.

At this moment she was remembering the voyage she had just made from Bombay with her father, Captain Crewe. She was thinking of the big ship, of the Lascars passing silently to and fro on it, of the children playing about on the hot deck, and of some young officers' wives who used to try to make her talk to them and laugh at the things she said.

Principally, she was thinking of what a queer thing it was that at one time one was in India in the blazing sun, and then in the middle of the ocean, and then driving in a strange vehicle through strange streets where the day was as dark as the night. She found this so puzzling that she moved closer to her father.

"Papa," she said in a low, mysterious little voice which was almost a whisper, "papa."

"What is it, darling?" Captain Crewe answered, holding her closer and looking down into her face. "What is Sara thinking of?"

"Is this the place?" Sara whispered, cuddling still closer to him. "Is it, papa?"

"Yes, little Sara, it is. We have reached it at last." And though she was only seven years old, she knew that he felt sad when he said it.

It seemed to her many years since he had begun to prepare her mind for "the place," as she always called it. Her mother had died when she was born, so she had never known or missed her. Her young, handsome, rich, petting father seemed to be the only relation she had in the world. They had always played together and been fond of each other. She only knew he was rich because she had heard people say so when they thought she was not listening, and she had also heard them say that when she grew up she would be rich, too. She did not know all that being rich meant. She had always lived in a beautiful bungalow, and had been used to seeing many servants who made salaams to her and called her "Missee Sahib," and gave her her own way in everything. She had had toys and pets and an ayah who worshipped her, and she had gradually learned that people who were rich had these things. That, however, was all she knew about it.

11. Based on the details in the passage, which of the following statements about Sara is true?
    A. *She is twelve years old.*
    B. *She used to live in India.*
    C. *She is a sailor.*
    D. *She is very familiar with London.*

12. Based on its usage in the first paragraph, which of the following is closest in meaning to the word "thoroughfares"?
    A. *parties*   B. *horses*   C. *streets*   D. *towns*

13. Where does the passage take place?
    A. *on a ship*   B. *in a shop*   C. *London*   D. *Bombay*

14. Based on the passage, which of the following best sums up Sara's character?
    A. *mature and thoughtful*   B. *young and stubborn*
    C. *smart and adventurous*   D. *scared and angry*

15. How is London described in the passage?
    A. *friendly and welcoming*   B. *busy and thrilling*
    C. *hot and sunny*   D. *dark and foggy*

16. Based on its usage in the second paragraph, which of the following is closest in meaning to the word "principally"?
    A. *mainly*   B. *strangely*   C. *naturally*   D. *carefully*

17. Based on the passage, how would you describe Sara's father?

    _____

    _____

18. How would you summarize this passage?

    _____

    _____

19. Based on its usage in the last paragraph, which of the following is closest in meaning to the word "bungalow"?
    A. *street lamp*   B. *cave*
    C. *single-story house*   D. *passenger ship*

20. According to the passage, what happened to Sara's mother?
    A. *She died when Sara was born.*
    B. *She died when Sara was seven.*
    C. *She died during the trip from Bombay.*
    D. *She is waiting for them in London.*

Read the paragraph and decide on the best word to fill each blank.

(1) If I could travel back into the past, I would _____ to see dinosaurs. (2) They were amazing creatures that _____ extinct millions of years ago. (3) Nobody knows what color _____ skin was, but it could have been very colorful. (4) Many modern reptiles have brightly colored patterns _____ their skin. (5) I _____ a bright green gecko that lives in a tank in my room.

21. In sentence 1, which word is the best choice to fill the blank?
    A. *wants*   B. *wanted*   C. *want*   D. *wanting*

22. In sentence 2, which word is the best choice to fill the blank?
    A. *went*   B. *gone*   C. *going*   D. *go*

23. In sentence 3, which word is the best choice to fill the blank?
    A. *there*   B. *they're*   C. *their*   D. *here*

24. In sentence 4, which word is the best choice to fill the blank?
    A. *with*   B. *through*   C. *by*   D. *on*

25. In sentence 5, which word is the best choice to fill the blank?
    A. *have*   B. *has*   C. *having*   D. *had*

26. Read this draft of a paragraph. Correct the grammar, punctuation, spelling, and capitalization.

The street next to the playground needs a stop sine so kids can use the park safely have you ever tried too cross the street in this spot? Its hard, especially on the Weekends when theirs more traffic. Also, even though the speed limit for cars is 25 miles per hour, much cars go faster. That scares kids who are plying in the park. A stop sign would make driver's slow down I think the town officials need to think seriously about installing a stop sign.

_____

_____

_____

_____

_____

_____

✓ Answer Key

Note: The answers to open-ended, constructed response questions are sample answers. Answers will vary, but look for the main ideas to be included.

Highlight any questions that your child gets wrong. Looking at the wrong answers may help to reveal one or more standards with which your child is struggling. Even if your child has done well on this post-test, reviewing the lessons will help him or her become a better reader and writer.

Passage	Question	Answer	Standard(s)
School Lunches	1	C	RI.4.2
	2	B	RI.4.4
	3	B	RI.4.1
	4	A	RI.4.4
	5	C	RI.4.3, RI.4.1
	6	D	RI.4.4
	7	D	RI.4.2
	8	Most problems with lunch programs involve a lack of money that can be invested in resolving the problem. This is true, whether the problem involves the kind of food served, the portions or lack of nutrients, or the price. Accept answers that are well-supported.	RI.4.2, RI.4.8, W.4.1
	9	A	RI.4.4
	10	According to the author, school lunches are important because they provide fuel for the body and brain.	RI.4.8
A Little Princess	11	B	RL.4.1
	12	C	RL.4.4
	13	C	RL.4.1
	14	A	RL.4.2
	15	D	RL.4.3
	16	A	RL.4.4
	17	Sara's father is a handsome, wealthy man who loves his daughter.	RL.4.3
	18	Sara journeys to London with her father for the first time. She finds it a strange place compared with her home in India. Though we don't know what will happen to Sara as the story continues, we know some important things: Sara's mother is dead, her father is rich, and she is arriving at a new place she has heard of many times.	RL.4.2
	19	C	RL.4.4
	20	A	RL.4.1
	21	C	W.4.5

Passage	Question	Answer	Standard(s)
	22	A	W.4.5
	23	C	W.4.5
	24	D	W.4.5
	25	A	W.4.5
	26	The street next to the playground needs a stop sign so kids can use the park safely. Have you ever tried to cross the street in this spot? It's hard, especially on the weekends when there's more traffic. Also, even though the speed limit for cars is 25 miles per hour, many cars go faster. That scares kids who are playing in the park. A stop sign would make drivers slow down. I think the town officials need to think seriously about installing a stop sign.	W.4.5

MATHEMATICS POST-TEST

1. Divide: 6,416 ÷ 7. Show your work using an area model.

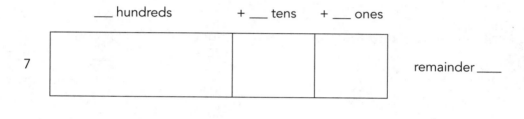

2. Find three fractions that are equivalent to $\frac{1}{3}$. Show your work.

3. Ahmad walks to school every morning and gets a ride home in the afternoon. The walk is 2 miles long and he goes to school 5 days a week. If he walks 3 miles on Saturday and stays home Sunday, then how many miles does he walk in a week?

4. A wall is painted red, blue, and green. If $\frac{2}{5}$ of the wall is red and $\frac{1}{5}$ of the wall is blue, then what fraction of the wall is green if all of the wall is painted?

A. $\frac{1}{5}$ B. $\frac{2}{5}$ C. $\frac{3}{5}$ D. $\frac{4}{5}$

5. When 107 is divided by 3, the quotient is 35 and the remainder is 2. Use this information to fill in the blanks and make the number sentence true: 107 = ___ × ___ + ___.

6. Which of the following is represented by the shaded region below?

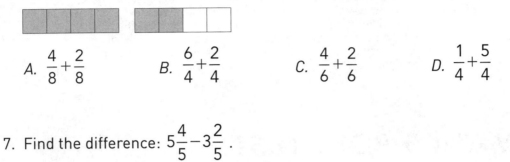

A. $\frac{4}{8}+\frac{2}{8}$ B. $\frac{6}{4}+\frac{2}{4}$ C. $\frac{4}{6}+\frac{2}{6}$ D. $\frac{1}{4}+\frac{5}{4}$

7. Find the difference: $5\frac{4}{5}-3\frac{2}{5}$.

8. Write an equation to represent the area model.

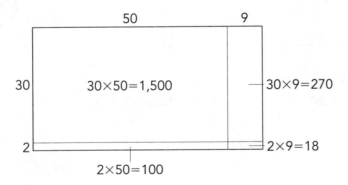

9. The closet in a classroom has boxes of pencils and each box contains 12 pencils. If there are a total of 96 pencils, then how many boxes are in the closet?
   A. 8   B. 10   C. 84   D. 108

10. Which of the following is equal to $12 \times \frac{1}{4}$?

A. $\frac{12}{4}$ B. $\frac{13}{4}$ C. $\frac{12}{48}$ D. $12\frac{1}{4}$

11. Brittney planted a tree. After 1 year, the tree had grown $10\frac{5}{7}$ inches. During the second year, the tree grew $8\frac{4}{7}$ inches. How many inches did the tree grow during its first two years?

    A. $18\frac{2}{7}$ B. 19 C. $19\frac{2}{7}$ D. $20\frac{1}{7}$

12. Which product can be found using $100 \times 5 + 2 \times 5$?
    A. 500×10 B. 200×10 C. 110×5 D. 102×5

13. Use $<$, $>$, or $=$ to make the number sentence true: $\frac{1}{3} \rule{1cm}{0.4pt} \frac{3}{6}$

14. A classroom has 4 rows of 6 desks. The teacher wants to put two pencils on each desk. If he has 19 pencils, how many more does he need?
    A. 1   B. 5   C. 19   D. 29

15. What fraction is equal to $4\frac{2}{6}$?

    A. $\frac{8}{6}$ B. $\frac{12}{6}$ C. $\frac{13}{3}$ D. $\frac{26}{3}$

16. Which of the following is equal to $\frac{3}{4}$?

    A. $3 \times \frac{1}{1}$ B. $3 \times \frac{1}{3}$ C. $3 \times \frac{1}{4}$ D. $3 \times \frac{3}{4}$

17. Which fraction is greater than $\frac{5}{8}$?

    A. $\frac{5}{12}$ B. $\frac{1}{2}$ C. $\frac{3}{4}$ D. $\frac{4}{10}$

18. Find the product: $10 \times \dfrac{2}{5}$

19. Which fraction is equal to $\dfrac{9}{8} + \dfrac{2}{8}$?

    A. $\dfrac{7}{8}$ B. $\dfrac{11}{8}$ C. $\dfrac{7}{16}$ D. $\dfrac{11}{16}$

20. What is the product of 3 and $\dfrac{2}{4}$?

    A. $\dfrac{5}{4}$ B. $\dfrac{6}{4}$ C. $\dfrac{5}{7}$ D. $\dfrac{6}{12}$

21. Using the area model, which equation is true?

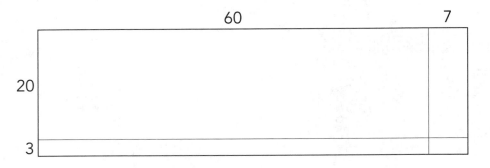

    A. $20 \times 60 = 20 \times 60 + 3 \times 7$

    B. $20 \times 60 \times 3 \times 7 = 1{,}200 \times 180 \times 140 \times 21$

    C. $23 \times 67 = 1{,}200 + 180 + 140 + 21$

    D. $23 \times 67 = 120 + 140 + 180 + 21$

22. There are 6 ribbons that are each $\dfrac{7}{8}$ meters long. How much ribbon is there, total?

23. Mr. Madden is using boxes to store his old games. If each box can hold 4 games, then how many boxes will he need if he has 18 games?

    A. 3   B. 4   C. 5   D. 6

24. Find the product of 3,241 and 6.

25. Which of the following fractions is equivalent to the shaded region below?

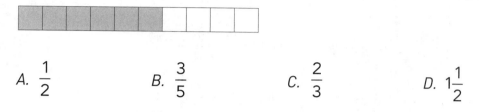

A. $\dfrac{1}{2}$ B. $\dfrac{3}{5}$ C. $\dfrac{2}{3}$ D. $1\dfrac{1}{2}$

 **Answer Key**

Question	Answer	Explanation	Standard
1	916 R 4	$\underline{9}$ hundreds $+ \underline{1}$ tens $+ \underline{6}$ ones; 7 │ 6,300 │ 70 │ 42 │ remainder $\underline{4}$	4.NBT.B.6
2	$2\dfrac{2}{5}$	$5\dfrac{4}{5}-3\dfrac{2}{5}=2\dfrac{4-2}{5}=2\dfrac{2}{5}$	4.NF.B.3c
3	19,446	$3241 \times 6 = 19446$	4.NBT.B.5
4	Sample answers: $\dfrac{2}{6}$, $\dfrac{3}{9}$, $\dfrac{4}{12}$	Equivalent fractions can be found by multiplying the numerator and the denominator by the same number.	4.NF.A.1
5	$\dfrac{1}{3}<\dfrac{3}{6}$	Since $\dfrac{2}{6}=\dfrac{1}{3}$, $\dfrac{3}{6}$ must be larger than $\dfrac{1}{3}$.	4.NF.A.1, 4.NF.A.2
6	$\dfrac{20}{5}$	$10\times\dfrac{2}{5}=\dfrac{20}{5}$	4.NF.B.4, 4.NF.B.4b
7	13	$2 \times 5 + 3 = 10 + 3 = 13$	4.OA.A.3
8	$107 = 35 \times 3 + 2$	By definition of the product, 35, and the remainder, $107 = 35 \times 3 + 2$.	4.NBT.B.4

Question	Answer	Explanation	Standard
9	$\dfrac{42}{8}$ m	$6 \times \dfrac{7}{8} = \dfrac{6 \times 7}{8} = \dfrac{42}{8}$	4.NF.B.4, 4.NF.B.4b, 4.NF.B.4c
10	$32 \times 59 = (30+2) \times (50+9)$	The total area of the rectangle is the length times the width. This can be represented in two ways, as shown with the given equation.	4.NBT.B.5
11	A	Using the general rule, $12 \times \dfrac{1}{4} = \dfrac{12 \times 1}{4} = \dfrac{12}{4}$.	4.NF.B.4, 4.NF.B.4a
12	D	Using place value methods, 102×5 can be found using 100×5 and adding it to 2×5	4.NBT.B.5
13	C	$4\dfrac{2}{6} = 4\dfrac{1}{3} = 1+1+1+1+\dfrac{1}{3} = \dfrac{3}{3}+\dfrac{3}{3}+\dfrac{3}{3}+\dfrac{3}{3}+\dfrac{1}{3} = \dfrac{13}{3}$	4.NF.A.1, 4.NF.B.3a
14	B	$3 \times \dfrac{2}{4} = \dfrac{3 \times 2}{4} = \dfrac{6}{4}$	4.NF.B.4, 4.NF.B.4b
15	C	$\dfrac{3}{4} = \dfrac{6}{8}$, therefore $\dfrac{3}{4} > \dfrac{5}{8}$	4.NF.A.2
16	D	There are $4 \times 6 = 24$ desks, so the teacher needs $24 \times 2 = 48$ pencils total. He has 19, so he still needs $48 - 19 = 29$ pencils.	4.OA.A.3
17	B	$\dfrac{9}{8} + \dfrac{2}{8} = \dfrac{9+2}{8} = \dfrac{11}{8}$	4.NF.B.3a, 4.NF.B.3b
18	C	The width of the rectangle is $20 + 3 = 23$ while the length is $60 + 7 = 67$. To find the total area, find the area of each rectangle: $20 \times 60 = 1{,}200$, $3 \times 60 = 180$, $20 \times 7 = 140$, $3 \times 7 = 21$, and then add: $1{,}200 + 180 + 140 + 21 = 1{,}541$.	4.NBT.B.5
19	B	The portion of the painting that is red and blue is $\dfrac{2}{5} + \dfrac{1}{5} = \dfrac{3}{5}$ and the remaining part is $\dfrac{5}{5} - \dfrac{3}{5} = \dfrac{2}{5}$.	4.NF.B.3d
20	C	$18 \div 4 = 4$ R 2, therefore he will need 5 boxes since 4 will leave 2 out	4.NBT.B.6
21	A	The total would be found by multiplying the number of boxes by 12. To find what number multiplied 12 to get 96, divide: $96 \div 12 = 8$.	4.NBT.B.6
22	C	$3 \times \dfrac{1}{4} = \dfrac{3 \times 1}{4} = \dfrac{3}{4}$	4.NF.B.4, 4.NF.B.4a